YES WE DID!

AMAZING ACCOMPLISHMENTS IN AFRICAN AMERICAN HISTORY

Jeffrey White
David Sanders

Yes We Did!

Jeffrey White and David Sanders

©2017
ISBN-13: 978-1978218222
ISBN-10: 1978218222
Jeff White Fitness Solutions
www.JeffWhiteFitnessSolutions.com
https://www.youtube.com/user/JWFitness1

Other Books by Jeffrey White:

The 3 Pillars of Strength: Increasing Your Physical, Mental, and Spiritual Fitness.

Readi, Set Go! A Simple Guide to Establishing a Successful Small Business.

Co-written with Stephanie Wynn

Success Principles 101: A Step By Step Guide on Setting and Achieving Goals.

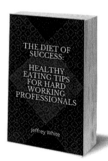

The Diet of Success: Healthy Eating Tips for Hard Working Professionals.

Dedication

Jeffrey White:

First, I'd like to thank God for blessing me and giving me the ability to write. I give all honor and thanks.

This book is dedicated to my mother, Patricia White-Sterling, my wife Monica, and Little Jeffrey, my son. My mother pushed me to become the best I can be, and my wife and son are my daily motivations to keep working hard. I hope to make you proud.

I must give a special thanks to my friend of over thirty years, the man responsible for the art seen in this book, David Sanders. Great work!

Lastly, this book is for those who are looking for more than what is shown in mainstream media and in traditional history books. Yes, there's much more out there, and we are determined to find it.

Dedication

David Sanders:

Special Thanks to God from whom my talents flow. My father and mother: Willie L. Sanders Sr. and Leaon Sanders (RIP). My Wife Shantay Mitchell- Sanders and my children Cyla, Tia, Elisha and granddaughter Cyliah. My stepmom Casirene Collins –Sanders (RIP). My siblings Willie Jr., Evelyn, Edward, Tony, Lamar and Jamar. Walter Mitchell Jr. and Marcus Mitchell who always got my back. June Latham my heart (RIP). My art teacher Mr. Sherman Beck who taught me that its's better to take my time and be satisfied than to rush for a profit. My spiritual family who taught me faith and Mr. Jeff White who has been a friend forever! There are more but I only have so much space!

This book is also dedicated to all young African Americans. This is proof that you can accomplish anything you set your mind to if you believe in yourself and the power of teamwork!!

Contents

Section I: African American Inventors

African Americans have played a major role in the history of the United States since its inception. Unfortunately, their contributions are often minimized or omitted altogether from standard history books. This does our society a disservice, as all contributions should be acknowledged and celebrated.

Many items we use today were created or improved by African American scientists and inventors. Here are a just a few of their amazing accomplishments.

1. Benjamin Banneker (November 9, 1731 – October 9, 1806)

"I am of the African race, and in the colour which is natural to them of the deepest dye; and it is under a sense of most profound gratitude to the Supreme Ruler of the Universe." Benjamin Banneker

Benjamin Banneker was born on November 9, 1731. His mother, (Mary) was a free black woman, and his father, (Robert) was a freed slave from the Republic of Guinea.

Banneker's grandmother, (Molly Welsh) was a woman from England, who in 1683, was sent to America as an indentured servant. This was her punishment for allegedly stealing milk from a farmer.

Upon arriving in America, Molly worked on a Maryland tobacco plantation for seven years. After earning her freedom in 1690, she purchased 120 acres of farmland on the outskirts of Baltimore, Maryland. In 1692, she purchased two slaves. One was the son of an African chieftain named Banneka. Three years later, Molly freed Banneka and they were married. They had four children, including Mary: Benjamin Banneker's mother.

Banneker's father (Robert) was a slave when he met Mary, but Molly bought his freedom so he could wed her daughter. Benjamin was born shortly thereafter in 1731.

Molly was very close to her children and grandchildren. She noticed how intelligent young Benjamin was, and used the Bible to teach him how to read and write. She eventually sent him to an integrated, one room school near the farm to continue his studies.

Banneker went to that school for eight years, and this was the only formal schooling he had in his entire life. Everything he learned going forward was self-taught. This was not easy as books were very expensive at the time. He couldn't afford his own books until he was in his thirties', so he borrowed as many as he could. His favorite books were those focused on mathematics, history and literature.

In addition to excelling in mathematics, Banneker was also good with his hands. When he was 22, he built a large wooden clock. What made this clock so extraordinary is he did not have a similar clock to work from or copy. Instead, he built it by enlarging the dimensions of a small pocket watch. The majority of the clock was made from wood that he carved by hand, with just a few metal components.

This was the only clock of its kind in Maryland, and word of its existence spread quickly. People of all races traveled great distances to see if this masterpiece really existed. That talent allowed him to earn a living repairing clocks and watches for over thirty years.

In the 1780's, a 50 year old Banneker discovered a new passion: astronomy. His neighbor, a Quaker named George Ellicott, befriended him, loaning him a telescope, books on astronomy and other related equipment. Banneker would spend his days working on watches and tending the family farm. At night, he studied the stars, analyzing their path and predicting where they would be in the nighttime sky, weeks and months in advance.

His projections were correct: In 1789, Banneker predicted his first major astronomical event, a solar eclipse. He began selling almanacs that accurately predicted planetary alignments and even more eclipses. His almanacs were extremely popular, increasing his notoriety even more throughout the state and surrounding areas.

Banneker's math skills continued to improve, allowing him to make complex calculations quickly and with pinpoint accuracy. This is the reason he was recruited in 1791 to help create the boundaries of the nation's capital, Washington D.C. at the ripe age of sixty.

George Ellicott's cousin, Major Andrew Ellicott was appointed by the Secretary of State (future President Thomas Jefferson) to head the survey team. Hearing of Banneker's stellar reputation and expertise, he personally invited Banneker to participate in the project.

Banneker's exact role on the survey team has been debated: some historians believe he made astronomical observations at Jones Point in Alexandria, Virginia to determine the survey's starting point. Others claim he used a clock to match points on the ground with stars in the sky to establish boundaries.

Unfortunately, Banneker became ill and was forced to return home before the survey was completed. Several months later, he wrote a letter to Thomas Jefferson, requesting African Americans be treated fairly and equally.

An excerpt from the letter reads as follows:

 "... Sir, how pitiable is it to reflect, that altho you were so fully convinced of the benevolence of the Father of mankind, and of his equal and impartial distribution of those rights and privileges which he had conferred upon them, that you should at the same time counteract his mercies, in detaining by fraud and violence so numerous a part of my brethren under groaning captivity and cruel oppression, that you should at the Same time be found guilty of that most criminal act, which you professedly detested in others, with respect to your Selves."

Jefferson responded, writing the following reply:

Philadelphia, PA. Aug. 30. 1791.

"Sir,
I thank you sincerely for your letter of the 19th. instant and for the Almanac it contained. no body wishes more than I do to see such proofs as you exhibit, that nature has given to our black brethren, talents equal to those of the other colours of men, & that the appearance of a want of them is owing merely to the degraded condition of their existence both in Africa & America. I can add with truth that no body wishes more ardently to see a good system commenced for raising the condition both of their body & mind to what it ought to be, as fast as the imbecillity of their present existence, and other circumstance which cannot be neglected, will admit. I have taken the liberty of sending your almanac to Monsieur de Condorcet, Secretary of the Academy of sciences at Paris, and member of the Philanthropic society because I considered it as a document to which your whole colour had a right for their justification against the doubts which have been entertained of them.

I am with great esteem, Sir,
Your most obedt. humble servt.
Th. Jefferson"

Banneker made a strong impression on Jefferson, who spoke highly of him in a letter to French philosopher and mathematician Marquis de Condorcet:

"I am happy to be able to inform you that we have now in the United States a negro, the son of a black man born in Africa, and of a black woman born in the United States, who is a very respectable mathematician. I procured him to be employed under one of our chief directors in laying out the new federal city on the Patowmac, & in the intervals of his leisure, while on that work, he made an Almanac for the next year, which he sent me in his own hand writing, & which I inclose to you. I have seen very elegant solutions of Geometrical problems by him. Add to this that he is a very worthy & respectable member of society. He is a free man. I shall be delighted to see these instances of moral eminence so multiplied as to prove that the want of talents observed in them is merely the effect of their degraded condition, and not proceeding from any difference in the structure of the parts on which intellect depends."

Banneker's love of astronomy never waned. It is reported that as he aged, he would lay in the fields of his farm, watching the stars until dawn, up to his death in 1806.

Did You Know?

- Banneker's clock worked for more than 40 years, keeping perfect time

- Banneker was a bachelor his entire life and never married

- Banneker was buried in an unmarked grave

- For six years, Banneker's almanacs were printed and sold in Baltimore, Maryland; Philadelphia, Pennsylvania; Wilmington, Delaware; and in the Virginia cities of Alexandria, Petersburg and Richmond

- In 1977, a commemorative obelisk was erected near his grave

Benjamin Banneker Almanac Cover (1795)

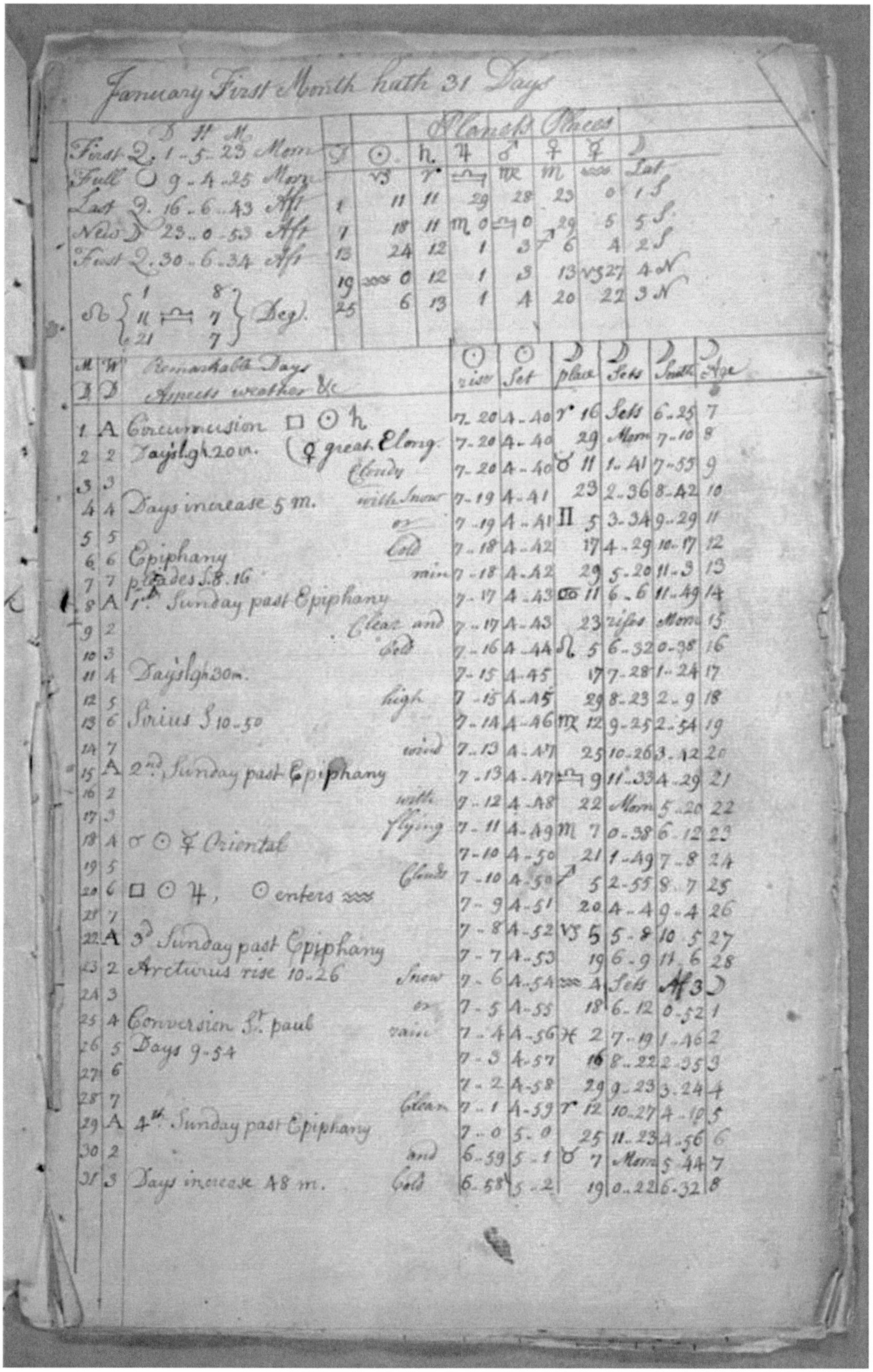

January First Month hath 31 Days

	D	H	M	
First ☽	1	5	23	Morn
Full ○	9	4	25	Morn
Last ☽	16	6	43	Aft
New ☽	23	0	53	Aft
First ☽	30	6	34	Aft

☊ {1, 11, 21} ♎ {8, 7, 7} (Deg).

Planets Places

D	☉	♄	♃	♂	♀	☿	☽ Lat
	♑	♈	♎	♍	♏	♒	
1	11	11	29	28	23	0	1 S
7	18	11	♏ 0	♎ 0	29	5	5 S
13	24	12	1	3	♐ 6	4	2 S
19	♒ 0	12	1	3	13	♑ 27	4 N
25	6	13	1	4	20	22	3 N

M D	W D	Remarkable Days Aspects weather &c		☉ rise	☉ Set	☽ place	☽ Sets	☽ South	☽ Age
1	A	Circumcision □ ☉ ♄		7-20	4-40	♈ 16	Sets	6-25	7
2	2	Dayslgh 20m. (☿ great Elong.		7-20	4-40	29	Morn	7-10	8
3	3		Cloudy	7-20	4-40	♉ 11	1-41	7-55	9
4	4	Days increase 5 m.	with Snow	7-19	4-41	23	2-36	8-42	10
5	5		or	7-19	4-41	♊ 5	3-34	9-29	11
6	6	Epiphany	Cold	7-18	4-42	17	4-29	10-17	12
7	7	pleiades S. 8.16	min	7-18	4-42	29	5-20	11-3	13
8	A	1st Sunday past Epiphany		7-17	4-43	♋ 11	6-6	11-49	14
9	2		Clear and	7-17	4-43	23	rises	Morn	15
10	3		Cold	7-16	4-44	♌ 5	6-32	0-38	16
11	4	Dayslgh 30m.		7-15	4-45	17	7-28	1-24	17
12	5		high	7-15	4-45	29	8-23	2-9	18
13	6	Sirius S 10-50		7-14	4-46	♍ 12	9-25	2-54	19
14	7		wind	7-13	4-47	25	10-26	3-42	20
15	A	2nd Sunday past Epiphany		7-13	4-47	♎ 9	11-33	4-29	21
16	2		with	7-12	4-48	22	Morn	5-20	22
17	3		flying	7-11	4-49	♏ 7	0-38	6-12	23
18	A	☌ ☉ ☿ Oriental		7-10	4-50	21	1-49	7-8	24
19	5		Clouds	7-10	4-50	♐ 5	2-55	8-7	25
20	6	□ ☉ ♃, ☉ enters ♒		7-9	4-51	20	4-4	9-4	26
21	7			7-8	4-52	♑ 5	5-8	10-5	27
22	A	3d Sunday past Epiphany		7-7	4-53	19	6-9	11-6	28
23	2	Arcturus rise 10-26	Snow	7-6	4-54	♒ 4	Sets	Aft 3	☽
24	3		or	7-5	4-55	18	6-12	0-52	1
25	4	Conversion St. paul	rain	7-4	4-56	♓ 2	7-19	1-46	2
26	5	Days 9-54		7-3	4-57	16	8-22	2-35	3
27	6			7-2	4-58	29	9-23	3-24	4
28	7		Clear	7-1	4-59	♈ 12	10-27	4-10	5
29	A	4th Sunday past Epiphany		7-0	5-0	25	11-23	4-56	6
30	2		and	6-59	5-1	♉ 7	Morn	5-44	7
31	3	Days increase 48 m.	Cold	6-58	5-2	19	0-22	6-32	8

Benjamin Banneker Almanac Contents (1795)

2. Dr. Patricia Bath (November 4th, 1942 -)

"Do not allow your mind to be imprisoned by majority thinking. Remember that the limits of science are not the limits of imagination." Dr. Patricia Bath

Dr. Patricia Bath is an African American ophthalmologist who revolutionized eye care by receiving a patent for her laser device that removed cataract lenses.

Dr. Bath was born in Harlem, New York. Her father, Rupert Bath was an immigrant from Trinidad and the first black man to work as a motorman on the New Yok City subway system. Her mother, Gladys Bath, was a homemaker who focused on raising the children.

Dr. Bath was given a microscope as a young child, which piqued her interest in math and science. She was extremely intelligent, graduating in just 2 years from Evans Hughes High School.

While still in high school, Bath won a National Science Foundation Scholarship. Upon receiving the scholarship, she completed a research project at Yeshiva University and Harlem Hospital. The project cited a link between nutrition, stress and certain forms of cancer. The teenager's findings were duly noted by the head of the research program, who published them in a scientific paper.

In 1964, Bath graduated from Hunter College, and studied at the Howard University School of Medicine. She also served as a fellow (period of medical training) at Columbia University. While interning in 1967, she traveled to Yugoslavia to further her studies.

It was on this trip that Bath decided to focus on children's health, with an emphasis on vision care. She also noticed how poor and black patients were not receiving adequate treatment and information on how to take care of their eyes. Determined to make a difference, she persuaded her professors from Columbia University to operate on blind patients at the Harlem Hospital Center for free.

The next year, she received her doctoral degree from Howard, becoming the first African American to serve her residency at New York University in ophthalmology.

After completing her residency, Dr. Bath held several prominent teaching positions:

- Assistant professor at Jules Stein Eye Clinic Institute at UCLA
- Professor of Ophthalmology at Howard University's School of Medicine
- Professor of Ophthalmology at St. George's University

Dr. Bath currently holds four patents in the United States. Her most famous is the Laserphaco Probe, which dissolves cataracts with a laser quickly and with little pain. It also cleans the eye and allows a new lens to be easily inserted.

Did you know?

- Dr. Bath was placed in the Hunter College "hall of fame", and was declared a "Howard University Pioneer in Academic Medicine" in 1993

- Dr. Bath was the first woman elected to the honorary staff at UCLA

- While still a teen, Bath won the Mademoiselle Magazine "Merit Award"

- Dr. Bath co-founded the American Institute for the Prevention of Blindness in 1978

- Dr. Bath is the first African American woman to receive a patent for medical purposes

- Dr. Bath was the first woman to head a residency in her field

United States Patent [19]

Bath

[11] **Patent Number:** **5,919,186**

[45] **Date of Patent:** *Jul. 6, 1999

[54] **LASER APPARATUS FOR SURGERY OF CATARACTOUS LENSES**

[76] Inventor: **Patricia E. Bath**, 4554 Circle View Blvd., Los Angeles, Calif. 90043

[*] Notice: This patent is subject to a terminal disclaimer.

[21] Appl. No.: **08/854,138**

[22] Filed: **May 8, 1997**

Related U.S. Application Data

[63] Continuation of application No. 07/717,794, Jun. 19, 1991, which is a continuation of application No. 07/159,931, Feb. 24, 1988, which is a division of application No. 06/943,098, Dec. 18, 1986, Pat. No. 4,744,350.

[51] Int. Cl.⁶ A61N 5/06

[52] U.S. Cl. 606/6; 606/3; 606/10; 606/15

[58] Field of Search 606/3–6, 10–18

[56] **References Cited**

U.S. PATENT DOCUMENTS

3,433,226	3/1969	Boyd .
3,971,383	7/1976	Krasnov .
3,982,541	9/1976	L'Esperance, Jr. .
4,320,761	3/1982	Haddad 604/22
4,538,608	9/1985	L'Esperance 606/5
4,583,539	4/1986	Karlin et al. 606/4
4,686,979	8/1987	Gruen et al. .
4,694,828	9/1987	Erchenbaum 606/6
4,744,360	5/1988	Bath .
5,324,282	6/1994	Dodick .
5,334,183	8/1994	Wuchinich .

OTHER PUBLICATIONS

C. Davis Belcher III, "The Future", *Ophthalmic Laser Therapy*, vol. 2, No. 4, 1987.

C. Davis Belcher III, "Phacoablation", *Ophthalmic Laser Therapy*, vol. 3, No. 1, 1988.

Gailitis et al., "Comparison of Laser Phacovaporization . . . ", '78/SPIE vol. 1744, *Ophthalmic Technologies II* (1992).

Primary Examiner—David M. Shay

[57] **ABSTRACT**

A method and apparatus for removing cataracts in which a flexible line preferably 1 mm or less in diameter is inserted through an incision into the anterior chamber until its end is adjacent the cataract. Coherent radiation, preferably at a frequency between 193 and 351 nm, is coupled to the cataract by an optical fiber in the line. An irrigation sleeve provided about the fiber and an aspiration sleeve extending partially around the irrigation sleeve conduct irrigating liquid to and remove ablated material from the anterior chamber and form with the optical fiber the flexible line.

17 Claims, 1 Drawing Sheet

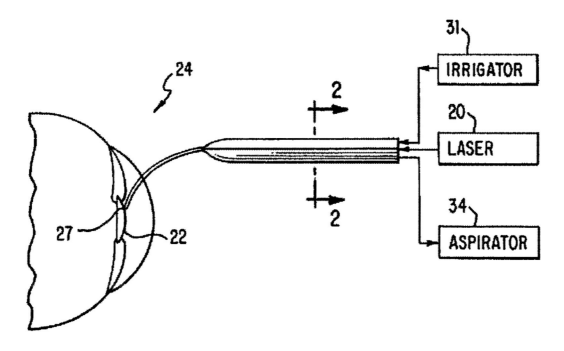

Dr. Patricia Bath Laser Apparatus for Surgery of Cataract Lenses Patent (1999)

3. George Carruthers (October 1, 1939 -)

"Failure is not in your vocabulary; rather, you convert all your working experiences, be they positive or negative, into fuel for future success." George Carruthers

Even as a young child, George Carruthers knew what his calling was: science and astronomy. Little did he know that years later, his love of the stars would be instrumental in the NASA space program, and his work would be admired by millions of people around the world.

Carruthers was born in Cincinnati, Ohio in 1939. He moved to Chicago, Illinois with his mother after his father (a civil engineer) passed away. Carruthers enjoyed the rich heritage Chicago offered, frequently visiting the various museums, libraries and the world-famous Adler Planetarium. Visiting the planetarium fueled his desire for astronomy even more, prompting him to become a member of the Chicago Rocket Society.

After graduating from Englewood High School on Chicago's south side, Carruthers continued his studies at the University of Illinois. In 1961, he graduated with a bachelor's of science degree in aeronautical engineering.

Carruthers continued to work hard, earning a master's degree in nuclear engineering and a doctorate in aeronautical and astro-nautical engineering in 1964.

After graduation, Carruthers moved to Washington D.C., where he worked for the Naval Research Laboratory. While working at the Lab, he focused on ultraviolet astronomy, which is the observation of electromagnetic radiation at ultraviolet wavelengths.

Ultraviolet light is not visible to the human eye, and can only be observed high in the atmosphere, above the earth, or from outer space. To help detect that electromagnetic radiation, Carruthers created the "Image Converter," and received a patent for his invention on November 11, 1969.

Thanks to his invention, a major milestone was accomplished just one year later: he made the first examination of molecular hydrogen in space.

In addition to the Image Converter, Carruthers is credited with the following:

- **The Far Violet Camera/Spectograph.** This is the first moon-based observatory, which Carruthers invented in 1972.

   - Placed on the moon on April 16, 1972 by Apollo 16 astronauts John Young and Charles Duke, the Spectograph was a combination telescope and camera that captured astronomical images of the electromagnetic spectrum. It produced never before seen images of stars, nebulas, and galaxies, as well as new images of planet earth.

     When asked about the Spectograph, Carruthers replied:

"This allows more accurate measurements of the compositions of interstellar gas, planetary atmospheres, etc. The ultraviolet also conveys important information on solid particles in interstellar space... and provides for much more accurate measurements of the energy output of very hot stars..."

- **Space Shuttle.** Carruthers invented a camera that was used on 1991 space shuttle missions.

Carruthers has made efforts to inspire the young and teach anyone interested about astronomy and science as well:

- o **The Science & Engineers Apprentice Program.** A summer program that invited high school students to work side by side with scientists at the Naval Research Library.

- o **D.C. Schools.** In the summers of 1996 & 1997, Carruthers taught a course on Earth and Space Science for D.C. Public Schools Science teachers.

- o **Howard University.** Carruthers taught a two semester course at Howard University, sponsored by the NASA Aerospace Workforce Development Grant.

Did you know?

- Carruthers struggled with math and physics as a child

- In 2013, Carruthers received the National Medal of Technology and Innovation from President Barack Obama

- NASA awarded Carruthers the Exceptional Achievement Scientific Award medal in 1972

- Carruthers was inducted into the National Inventors Hall of Fame in 2003

- An ultraviolet image of Haley's Comet was captured using one of Carruthers inventions in 1986

Nov. 11, 1969   G. R. CARRUTHERS   3,478,216
        IMAGE CONVERTER FOR DETECTING ELECTROMAGNETIC RADIATION
                   ESPECIALLY IN SHORT WAVE LENGTHS
                          Filed July 27, 1966

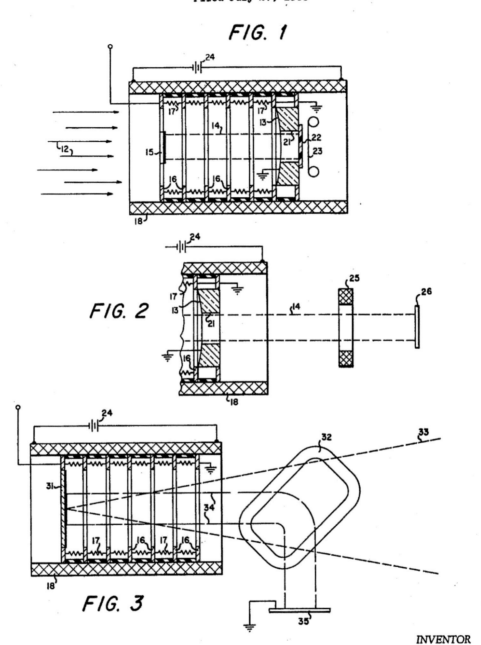

George Carruthers Image Converter Patent (1969)

4. George Washington Carver (1861? – January 5, 1943)

"How far you go in life depends on your being tender with the young, compassionate with the aged, sympathetic with the striving and tolerant of the weak and strong. Because someday in your life you will have been all of these."

"Ninety-nine percent of the failures come from people who have the habit of making excuses."

"Education is the key to unlock the golden door of freedom." George Washington Carver

Even though he was born a slave in Missouri, George Washington Carver's keen intelligence and ingenuity helped revolutionize agriculture in the South and around the world.

Carver didn't know either of his parents: his father was killed before he was born, and when he was an infant, he, his mother and sister were kidnapped and taken to Kentucky, where they were sold. Only George was rescued and returned to the plantation. He never heard from his mother or sister again.

Carver was unable to work in the fields because he was weak and somewhat sickly. As a result, he was relegated to indoor duties. This is when he began his fascination with plants and drawing.

Carver was owned by Moses Carver, an immigrant from Germany who noticed young George's intense desire to learn. When slavery was abolished in 1865, Moses and his wife taught Carver to read. They also encouraged him to continue learning as much as he could.

This was easier said than done. The quest for Carver to get an education was full of roadblocks and setbacks:

- Carver couldn't go to public school in Diamond Grove Missouri, so at the tender age of twelve, he left the Moses' home and attempted to go to school 10 miles away in Neosho, Missouri. There, he met Mariah Watkins, who took him in.

  According to Carver, she told him: *"You must learn all you can, then go back out into the world and give your learning back to the people".*

- At the age of thirteen, he witnessed an African American man attacked and killed by an angry mob. Seeing this prompted him to change schools and live with another foster family in Fort Scott, Kansas.

- After earning a diploma at Minneapolis High School in Minneapolis, Kansas, he was accepted to Highland University in Highland Kansas. Unfortunately, when they realized he was African American, they rescinded their acceptance.

Carver wasn't about to give up. That just made him more determined, prompting him to work even harder.

Undaunted, he quickly applied to Simpson College in Indianola, Iowa and was accepted. While studying, he discovered he had a passion for science, so he transferred to Iowa Agricultural College (now known as Iowa State University).

Carver graduated with a Bachelor's of Science degree in 1894. Two years later, he earned his Master of Science in Bacterial Botany and Agriculture. Dr. Carver was an exceptional student, and was given the opportunity to become the first black faculty member at Iowa College.

Shortly thereafter, Carver was invited by Booker T. Washington to become director of the department of Agriculture at the Tuskegee Normal and Industrial Institute. (Washington was the president of the school at the time.) He also became a teacher at the college.

While at Tuskegee, Carver amassed an amazing list of accomplishments and inventions:

- Created innovative techniques to improve soils depleted from the planting of cotton
- Helped implement the practice of crop-rotation, which helped restore much-needed nitrogen in the soil
- Created house paint from pigments of clay
- Produced paper from wood shavings
- Discovered methods to turn soybeans into plastics
- Discovered approximately 300 uses for the peanut

As Carver's work became known across the South, his popularity increased dramatically. In 1920, the United Peanut Associations of America invited Carver to speak at their convention, where he showcased 145 of the peanut products he invented.

Carver only has 3 patents on record with the U.S. patent office, but in his personal journals, he lists the following inventions and innovations as his creations:

- 73 dyes
- 17 wood fillers
- 14 candies
- 5 library pastes
- 5 breakfast foods
- 4 starches
- 4 flours
- 3 molasses

A proud and honorable Christian man, Carver created eight cardinal virtues that he shared with his students while teaching at Tuskegee:

1. Always be considerate of women, children, and older people.
2. Be too brave to lie.
3. Be too generous to cheat.
4. Take your share of the world and let others take theirs.

5. Be clean both inside and out.
6. Neither look up to the rich nor down on the poor.
7. Lose, if need be, without squealing.
8. Win without bragging.

Carver died on January 5, 1943 at the age of 78 after falling down a flight of stairs. The following was written on his grave:

"He could have added fortune to fame, but caring for neither, he found happiness and honor in being helpful to the world."

Did you know?

- On May 7, 1943, the Liberty Ship SS George Washington Carver was launched

- The USS George Washington Carver, a nuclear powered, fleet ballistic missile submarine was launched on August 14, 1965

- Carver was the first black student to attend Iowa State Agricultural College in 1891

- In 1916, Carver was made a member of the Royal Society of Arts, based in England

- Presidents Theodore Roosevelt, Calvin Coolidge and Franklin D. Roosevelt all consulted with Carver and sought his opinions on farming and agriculture

- Because his exact date of birth is unknown, the US Congress named January 5th (the date of his death) George Washington Carver Recognition Day in 1943

- Carver was featured on a 50 cents coin by the U.S. Mint from 1951-1954

- In 1941, Time Magazine called Carver a *"Black Leonardo"* (da Vinci)

- Carver was a member of Phi Beta Sigma fraternity incorporated

Patented June 9, 1925.

1,541,478

UNITED STATES PATENT OFFICE.

GEORGE W. CARVER, OF TUSKEGEE, ALABAMA.

PAINT AND STAIN AND PROCESS OF PRODUCING THE SAME.

No Drawing.   Application filed June 13, 1923.   Serial No. 645,199.

To all whom it may concern:

Be it known that I, GEORGE W. CARVER, a citizen of the United States, residing at Tuskegee, in the county of Macon and State of Alabama, have invented certain new and useful Improvements in Paints and Stains and Processes of Producing the Same, of which the following is a specification.

The invention relates to paints and stains, and has as an object the provision of a process for producing paints and stains from clays. Clays are found in many sections of the country of a variety of colors, and by a proper choice of color there may be produced by the process of the invention a large variety of colors of pigments, fillers and stains for treating wood or other materials.

To carry out the process of the invention the desired clay having a high percentage of iron is treated by any of the well known processes for refining the same and reducing it to a finely divided condition. A desirable composition for a clay to be treated by the process of the present invention is 5.6% peroxide of iron and 16.7% aluminum.

While a clay testing as above described and substantially free from lime or any similar alkali is suitable for the carrying out of the process, yet a higher iron content will vary the effect only by improving the result.

To reduce the clay to a gelatinous condition the same is treated with acid. For this purpose taking as a basis a quantity of 25 pounds of clay free from sand or other objectionable substances, 25 pounds of commercial sulphuric acid and 25 pounds commercial hydrochloric acid may be added to the clay, with three pounds of clean scrap iron of any kind, iron turnings being a desirable form for the iron. The clay and iron are put into an acid-proof vessel which is capable of withstanding heat, as for instance a porcelain vessel. The acids are added with enough water to make a thin paste. The substance is then boiled slowly, with frequent stirring, until the iron is dissolved, and the whole mass assumes a uniform color.

Water free from alkali is then added sufficient to substantially double the volume, when the solution is well stirred and allowed to settle for about five minutes, for the purpose of settlement of coarser portions. The material remaining in suspension with the liquid is then decanted into shallow acid-proof vessels and the remaining coarse and insoluble material is thrown away.

The material thus secured is utilized as a base for subsequent steps, the nature of which, as well as the nature of the clay first taken for treatment may be chosen to vary the color of the resultant products.

As a variation of the above process the nitric acid may be added with the sulphuric and hydrochloric, but it is found that slightly inferior results are thus obtained. Moreover copperas may be substituted for the scrap iron with, however, probably not such fine results.

For use as a wood filler or stain, clay of a desired color may be treated with the acid as above described, and the thus secured gelatinous clay is found to strike into the wood fiber and to produce an exceedingly smooth surface, giving a color thereto dependent upon the color of clay chosen for treatment, thereby acting as a filler and stain with the single application. It is found that a filler made as thus described becomes very hard when dry and enables the wood to take a high polish. Moreover specimens of wood which have been thus treated are found, after twenty years, to be brighter and more beautiful than when first treated. For this use the iron scrap may be omitted if desired.

The material thus described as a compound filler and stain, may be dried and mixed with linseed oil or its equivalent as a pigment to provide a paint. If desired to be darkened to a slight extent some good grade of carbon or lamp black may be added.

When the above acid treatment is carried out utilizing a micaceous clay of the variety of shades which occur in the Southern States a sheen results that has not to my knowledge been secured by heretofore used artificial mixtures.

I claim:

1. The process of producing pigment or the like which comprises boiling clay and metallic iron with acid and separating the coarser particles therefrom.

2. The process of producing pigments or the like which comprises boiling a mixture of clay and scrap iron with a mixture of sulphuric and hydrochloric acid, and separating the coarser particles therefrom, the color of clay utilized being chosen in accordance with the color desired in the finished product.

GEORGE W. CARVER.

5. George Speck (July 15, 1824? – July 22, 1914)

"Pass the chips and salsa."

Who was George Speck? It depends on who you ask. Also known as George Crum, he was born in Saratoga County, located in New York State. His father (Abraham) was African American, while his mother (Diana) was Native American. Some historians claim he's a descendant of African Americans and possibly Oneida, Stockbridge and possibly Mohawk tribes. Others believe they are from the Regis (Akwesasne) Mohawk reservation.

While the debate about Crum's ancestry may never be resolved, there is one thing everyone can agree on: Crum was a master chef who revolutionized one of the world's most popular snacks: the potato chip.

Before becoming a chef, Crum worked as a tour guide in the Adirondack Mountains and as an animal trapper. In 1853, he started working exclusively as a chef at the Moons Lake House restaurant at the Saratoga Lakes Resort. Moons Lake House was a high-end, fancy restaurant frequented by many wealthy patrons. His sister Katie worked with him in the restaurant as well.

It should be noted that Crum did *not* invent the potato chip. He accidentally created a variation that would become more popular than the original version:

One day, while working at Moon's Lake, a customer complained about the potato slices he received from Crum, and sent them back to the kitchen. Crum was a well-known chef at the time, with patrons traveling great distances to eat his delicious meals.

Crum was reportedly offended by the gesture, so out of spite, he cut the potato into the thinnest slices he could, cooked them longer normal, and added extra salt as well.

Crum was hoping to upset the customer, but the exact opposite happened: *he loved them.* On that day, Saratoga Chips was born.

In 1860, Crum opened his own upscale restaurant: Crum's House in Malta, New York. His chips continued to be extremely popular, and were served on every table.

Did you know?

- Crum's House catered to wealthy, affluent customers. Some of his regular patrons included the following:

    - Railroad tycoon William Vanderbilt (the richest man in America)
    - Wealthy businessman Henry Hilton
    - Railroad developer and speculator Jay Gould

- Some historians believe Crum's sister Katie actually discovered the new version of the potato chip when she accidentally dropped a potato slice into the fryer

- Crum never patented his idea - It is rumored that Herman Lay took Crum's version of the potato chip across the United States, increasing its popularity and using it to start his Lay's potato chips brand

George Crum's Saratoga Chips

6. Charles R. Drew (June 3, 1904 – April 1, 1950)

"I feel that the recent ruling of the United States Army and Navy regarding the refusal of colored blood donors is an indefensible one from any point of view. As you know, there is no scientific basis for the separation of the bloods of different races except on the basis of the individual blood types or groups." Charles R Drew

Charles Richard Drew was born in Washington, D.C. He graduated from Dunbar High School and received an athletic scholarship from Amherst College in Massachusetts. After graduating in 1926, he studied medicine at McGill University in Montreal, Quebec, receiving his Medicinae Doctorem et Chirurgiae Magistrum (MDCM) in 1933.

Dr. Drew went on to earn his Doctor of Medical Science degree from Columbia University, quickly earning the reputation among his peers as a highly intelligent, well respected physician. Dr. Drew became the first African American surgeon selected to serve as an examiner on the American Board of Surgery.

Revolutions in Medicine

In 1940, Dr. Drew received an interesting request: Dr. John Scudder, a blood transfusion specialist, enlisted him to help develop a program for blood storage and preservation. The program, called *Blood for Britain,* was designed with the hopes of delivering blood donations from the United States to civilians and British soldiers in the United Kingdom.

Dr. Drew agreed to work on the project, and his ingenuity led to the creation of what is known today as the bloodmobile, which is the process of storing refrigerated containers of blood in trucks.

The Blood for Britain program was deemed a tremendous success, which led to the creation of the American Red Cross Blood Bank and revolutionized the use of Bloodmobiles across the United States.

Did you know?

- Dr. Charles Drew was a member of Omega Psi Phi fraternity Incorporated

- A park in Quebec is named after Dr. Drew (Parc Charles-Drew)

- Dr. Drew was the first African American to earn a Doctor of Medical Science degree from Columbia University

- The U.S. Navy christened and launched the USNS Charles Drew cargo ship on February 27, 2010

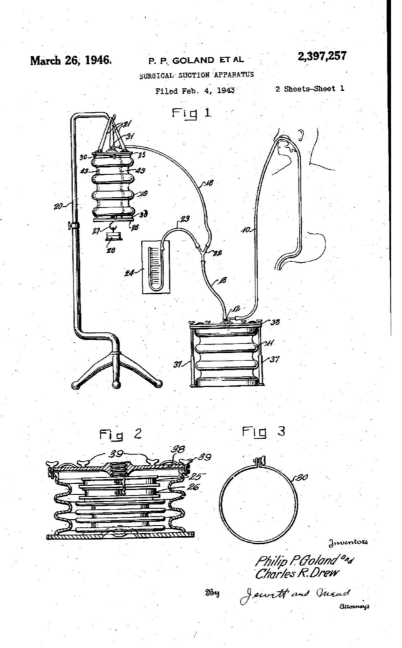

Charles Drew Surgical Suction Apparatus Patent (1946)

7. Thomas Elkins (unknown)

Little is known about Thomas Elkins' personal life, but his inventions should make him a household name.

Thomas Elkins was a pharmacist who had a keen eye for taking common household products and making them better:

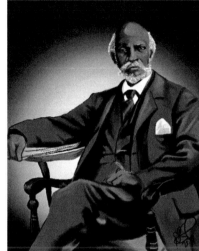

Ironing table. On February 22, 1870, Elkins received his first patent, which was for his combination dining table, ironing table and quilting frame (patent #100020). This invention was ideal for those in cramped living spaces.

Chamber Commode. Just two years later on January 9, 1872, Elkins received his second patent: the chamber commode (patent #122518). Also designed for those with limited space, it was a combination toilet, bureau, table, easy chair, mirror, book rack and wash stand. Previously, these were all separate items, but Elkins discovered a way to combine them into one smoothly functioning unit.

Refrigerating apparatus. Elkins most famous patent was received seven years later, on November 4, 1879 (patent #221222). The first refrigeration machine was created by Oliver Evans in 1805. Elkins' patent was for the insulated cabinet that held the ice, helping keep the refrigerator cool.

Did you know?

- Thomas Elkins was an abolitionist and the secretary of the Vigilance Committee. The Committee provided temporary shelter for fugitives seeking freedom. They also provided food, clothing, money and legal counsel if needed.

- The refrigerating apparatus was not only used for food, it was also used as a body cooling chamber. This helped prevent the spread of disease, and was used as storage until bodies could be buried.

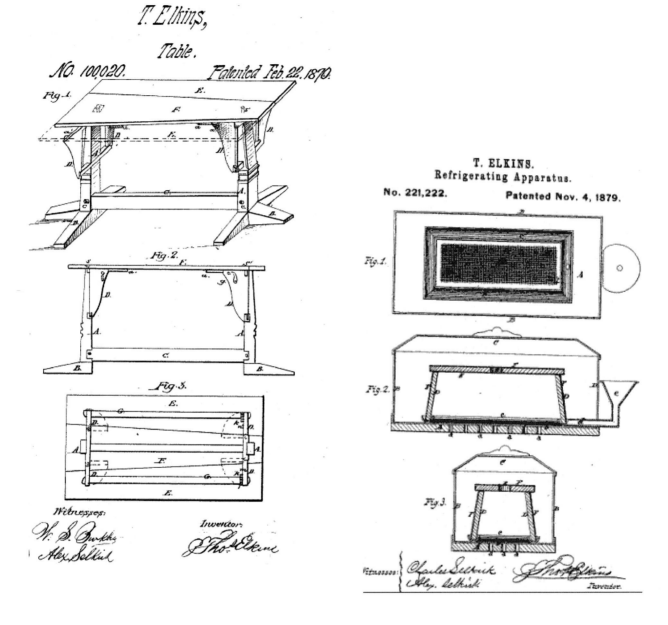

Thomas Elkins Ironing Table (1870) and Refrigerating Apparatus Patents (1879)

8. Thomas L. Jennings (1791? – February 12, 1856)

On March 3, 1821, Thomas Jennings made history as the first African American to ever receive a patent for an invention.

Jennings was born a free man in New York City. Not much is known about Jennings's childhood except he learned to become a tailor at an early age. He was known for doing excellent work, eventually opening his own shop in New York City.

Jennings noticed how many of his customers would complain about stains ruining their clothes and the material. Sensing a unique business opportunity, Jennings began experimenting with various chemicals in an effort to remove stains without damaging the clothing. In 1821, his "dry scouring process" was created, and patent 3306x was granted to him on March 3 of that same year.

Jennings' patent made him a very wealthy man, which was instrumental in a court case involving his daughter, Elizabeth Jennings:

In 1854, Elizabeth was forcibly removed from a streetcar and arrested. Jennings filed a lawsuit, hiring the powerful law firm Culver, Parker and Arthur to sue the bus company. Jennings eventually won the case, receiving $225.00 and $22.50 in costs. The case was represented in court by a young attorney named Chester Arthur. Arthur would go on to achieve history himself, becoming the 21st President of the United States.

Did you know?

- Jennings used the monies received from his patent to buy his family member's freedom

- Modern day dry cleaning is based on Jennings's Dry Scouring technique

- In 1855, Jennings organized the Legal Rights Association, which organized legal defense for African Americans

- Jennings founded the Abyssinian Baptist Church in Harlem and was a trustee

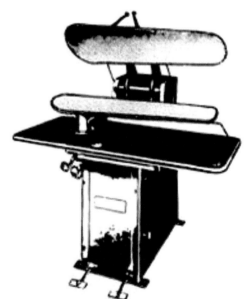

9. Katherine Johnson (August 26, 1918 -)

"I felt most proud of the success of the Apollo mission. They were going to the moon and I computed the path to get there." Katherine Johnson

Mathematician Katherine Johnson played one of the most important roles in the history of NASA: as millions of people around the world watched with baited breath, it was her calculations that allowed Alan Shepard, the first American to be launched into space, reenter the earth's atmosphere at the perfect trajectory, allowing him to land safely on May 5, 1961.

Katherine Johnson is the star of the movie *Hidden Figures,* based on the book by Margot Lee Shetterly. The book chronicles the true story of Johnson and fellow African American mathematicians Mary Jackson and Dorothy Vaughn. Taraji Henson played Johnson in the film that was released in 2016.

Johnson was born on August 26, 1918 in White Sulphur Springs, West Virginia. Her father (Joshua Coleman) was a farmer and handyman, while her mother (Joylette Coleman) was a school teacher.

Johnson's parents recognized early on that she was highly intelligent, far beyond her years. Math came easy for her, as she solved complex math problems with little difficulty. Since the county they lived in only had schooling for African Americans up to 8th grade, Johnson and her siblings went to high school in nearby Institute, West Virginia.

Johnson was only ten years old when she started high school.

After graduating high school at age 14, she attended West Virginia State College, a historically black college (HBCU) now known as West Virginia State University, where she continued to excel in math.

At age 18, Johnson graduated from college in 1937 with degrees in French and mathematics. She was summa cum laude, which means *"with praise"* or *"with honor"* in Latin. In most U.S. schools, this distinction is reserved for students who graduate in the top 5% to 10% of their class.

After marrying and starting a family, Johnson worked as a teacher. In 1952, she was told that the National Advisory Committee for Aeronautics (NACA) was hiring mathematicians. NACA was created in 1915, and its mission was to *"undertake, promote, and institutionalize aeronautical research"*. In 1958 the agency was disbanded, and the National Aeronautics and Space Administration (NASA) was created, taking its place.

Johnson was offered the position in 1953 and worked with other women of color performing math calculations. At the time, African Americans had to use separate restrooms, as well as eat and work in segregated areas. Johnson eventually worked in the Guidance and Control Division of Langley's Flight Research Division. She was the only African American woman in the department.

Even though segregation still existed at NASA and around the country, Johnson was very outspoken and stood up for herself:

"We needed to be assertive as women in those days – assertive and aggressive – and the degree to which we had to be that way depended on where you were. I had to be. In the early days of NASA women were not allowed to put their names on the reports – no woman in my division had had her name on a report.

"I was working with Ted Skopinski and he wanted to leave and go to Houston ... but Henry Pearson, our supervisor – he was not a fan of women – kept pushing him to finish the report we were working on. Finally, Ted told him, 'Katherine should finish the report, she's done most of the work anyway.' So Ted left Pearson with no choice; I finished the report and my name went on it, and that was the first time a woman in our division had her name on something."

Johnson spent the bulk of her career at NASA in the Spacecraft Controls Branch. One of the many highlights of her stellar career was her interaction with the famous astronaut, John Glenn:

John Glenn was the first American to orbit the earth, circling it three times in 1962. Even though NASA used computers to calculate the rocket's trajectory, Glenn refused to start the mission until Johnson herself double-checked those same numbers and verified them by hand.

Did you know?

- Katherine Johnson created backup navigation plots for astronauts in case of electronic failures

- In 1969, Johnson helped calculate the Apollo 11 flight to the moon

- When the Apollo 13 moon mission was aborted mid-flight in 1970, Johnson helped chart a hasty, improvised return to Earth

- Johnson has worked on the Space Shuttle Program and helped devise plans for future missions to Mars

- President Barack Obama presented Johnson with the Presidential Medal of Freedom in 2015

- Dedicated by NASA, The Katherine G. Johnson Computational Research Facility in Hampton, Virginia opened its doors on September 22, 2017

- Johnson won the NASA Langley Research Special Achievement award in 1971, 1980, 1984, 1985, and 1986

- One of Johnson's college mentors was W.W. Schieffin Claytor, the third African American to ever receive a Ph.D. in math

- When asked about the movie Hidden Figures, Johnson replied: *"It was well-done. The three leading ladies did an excellent job portraying us."*

10. John Lee Love (September 26, 1889 – December 26, 1931)

"Can I borrow your pencil sharpener?"

John Lee Love is from Fall River, Massachusetts. Not much is known about his life, other than the fact that he was a carpenter. On November 23, 1897, he received patent #594114 for the pencil sharpener.

Did you know?

- Love's invention was called the "Love Sharpener"

- In 1895, Love received a patent for an improved plasterers hawk, used by plasterers and masons

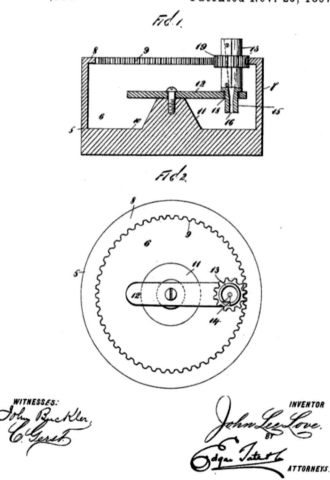

John Love Pencil Sharpener Patent (1897)

11. Alexander Miles (May 18, 1838 – May 7, 1918)

Going up? Three please!

Alexander Miles was born in Duluth, Minnesota and made a living by owning a barbershop. One day, while riding an elevator with his daughter, he noticed how the elevator shaft stayed open. (Originally, the opening and closing of both the shaft and elevator had to be completed manually.)

Seeing the dangers this could pose, Miles created a design for automatically opening and closing elevator doors through a series of levers and rollers. He received patent #371207 on October 11, 1887, and his design is still used in today's modern elevators.

In 1900, Alexander Miles was thought to be the *"wealthiest colored man in the Northwest."*

Did you know?

- Alexander Miles was inducted to the National Inventors Hall of Fame in 2007

- In 1900, Miles and his family moved to Chicago and created an insurance agency, in hopes of eliminating the discriminatory practices against people of color

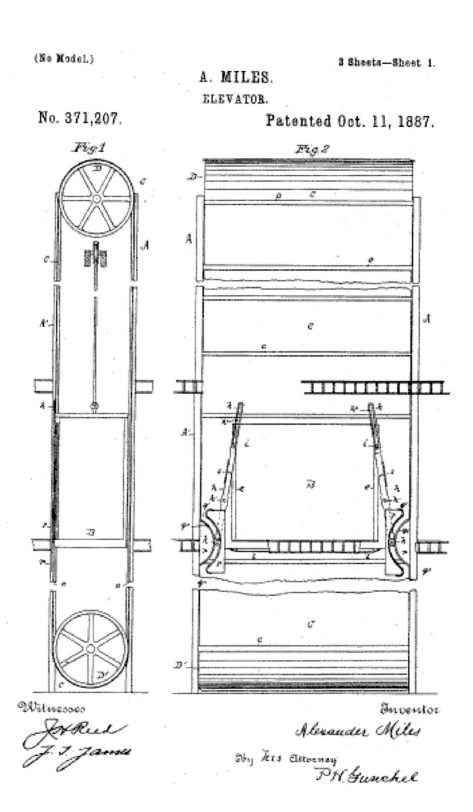

Alexander Miles Elevator Patent (1887)

12. Garrett A. Morgan (March 4, 1877 – July 27, 1963)

"If you can be the best, then why not try to be the best?" **Garrett A. Morgan**

Garrett A. Morgan was born in Paris, Kentucky in 1877. At age 16, he quit school, taking a full-time job repairing sewing machines for a clothing store in Cleveland, Ohio. He enjoyed his job and quickly discovered he had a knack for fixing things.

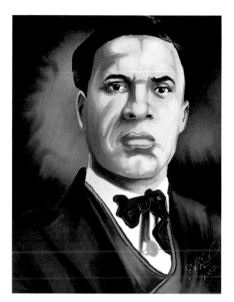

Even at a young age, Morgan was curious and very ambitious. He had big dreams and knew he wanted to do something with his life. In 1907, he opened his own sewing machine shop.

When Morgan wasn't working on his business, he was active in the community, helping form the Cleveland Association of Colored Men in 1908.

As his skills grew, so did his imagination and creativity: in 1912, he created first invention: a belt fastener for sewing machines.

The Smoke Hood

Morgan always knew he wanted to do more than repair sewing machines, so he created the *"smoke hood,"* receiving patent #1113675 on October 13, 1914. The inspiration to create the smoke hood came after seeing firefighters suffer from smoke inhalation when battling fires.

Today, the smoke hood is known as the gas mask.

After receiving his patent, Morgan created the National Safety Device Company, and began selling smoke hoods across the country. On July 24th, 1916, Morgan got his big break: A tunnel explosion under Lake Erie trapped many workers in the rubble. Firefighters attempted to enter the tunnel and rescue them, but the thick plumes of smoke forced them back.

After several failed rescue attempts, an urgent request was sent to Morgan for assistance. No one believed his product worked, so Morgan and his brother volunteered to rescue the trapped miners themselves. They strapped on their smoke hoods and fearlessly entered the tunnel. After several agonizing minutes, they emerged, unscathed, with the workers (still alive) to the cheers of relieved onlookers.

Word spread quickly about the success of Morgan's smoke hood and sales skyrocketed. Fire departments across the country placed orders for his invention and immediately put them to use. The smoke hood was so popular, Morgan was made an honorary member of the International Association of Firefighters.

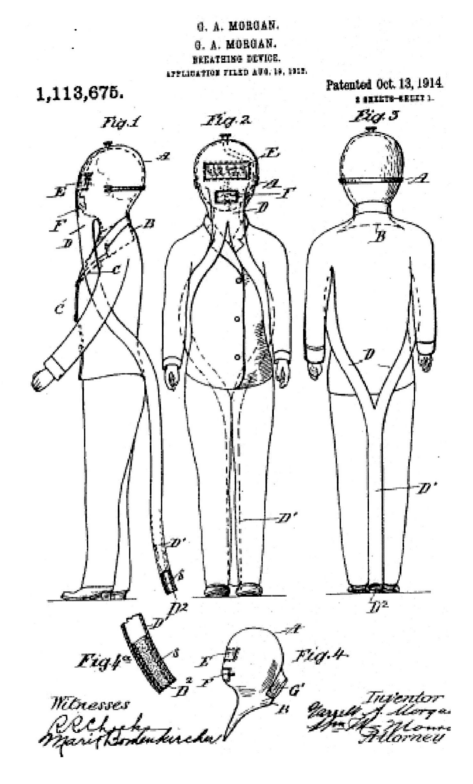

Garrett A. Morgan Smoke Hood Patent (1914)

Traffic Signal

The first variations of the traffic light originally had two signals: stop and go. However, after witnessing a terrible accident at an intersection, Morgan created the three-position traffic signal, receiving patent #1475024 on November 20, 1923. The new and improved traffic signal drastically decreased the number of accidents, and increased the safety of both drivers and pedestrians alike.

Did You Know?

- Morgan is an honorary member of Alpha Phi Alpha Fraternity Incorporated

- One of Morgan's last inventions was created after he developed glaucoma and was functionally blind: a self-extinguishing cigarette

- Morgan received a gold medal from the International Association of Fire Chiefs for the safety hood

- Morgan was a Prince Hall Freemason

- Morgan helped form an all-black country club in 1920, the Wakeman Country Club

- The U.S. Army provided smoke hoods to troops in World War I

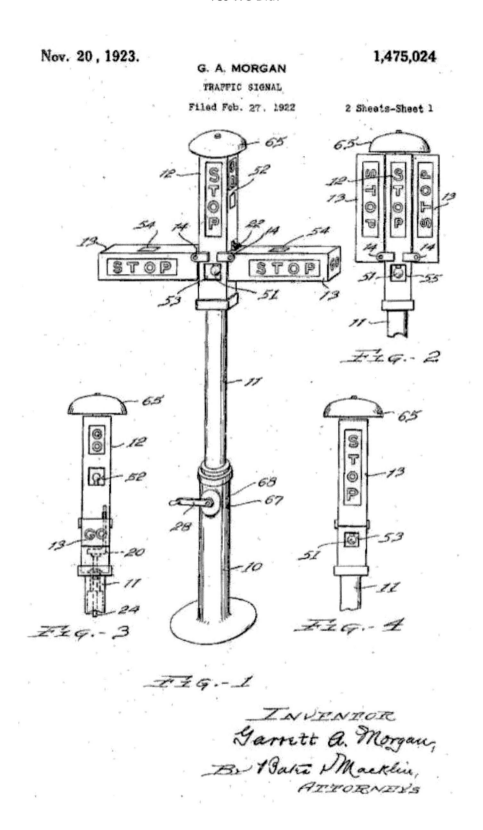

Garrett A Morgan Traffic Signal Patent (1923)

13. William B. Purvis (August 12, 1838 – August 10, 1914)

"The object of my invention is to provide a simple, durable, and inexpensive construction of a fountain pen adapted to general use and which may be carried in the pocket." **William B. Purvis**

William Purvis was a man looking to make things easier. Instead of complaining and waiting on someone else to do something, he took it upon himself to make improvements to many of the world's most commonly used products.

The fountain pen. If a person wanted to use a fountain pen in the 1800's, they had to carry a bottle of ink with them. (Not only was this inconvenient, it could be very messy.) On January 7, 1890, the fountain pen was born (patent #419065). The ink would now be contained in a reservoir within the pen.

Carrying a bottle of ink was a hindrance to learning how to write, because not everyone had the luxury of carrying ink everywhere they went. Now that more people had access to fountain pens, their ability (and desire) to learn how to write increased literacy rates dramatically.

Did you know?

The improvement to the fountain pen is Purvis' most popular invention, but he has several other patents on record as well:

- **Bag fastener.** Patent #256856. 4/25/1882

- **Hand stamp.** Patent #273149 2/27/1885

- **Paper bag machine.** Patent #460093 9/22/1891

- **Electric railway.** Patent #588176 5/1/1894

- **Magnetic Car Balancing Device.** Patent #539542 5/21/1895

- **Electric railway switch.** Patent #588176 8/17/1897

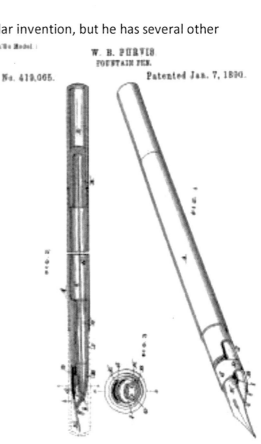

W.B. Purvis Fountain Pen Patent (1890)

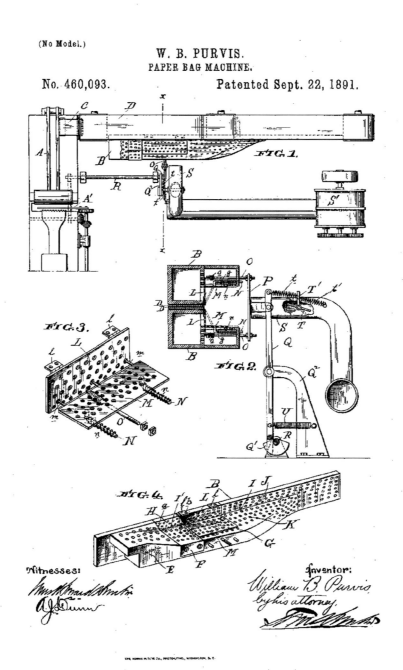

W.B. Purvis Paper Bag Machine Patent (1891)

14. John Standard (June 15, 1868 – unknown)

"This invention relates to improvements in refrigerators; and it consists of certain novel arrangements and combinations of parts." John Standard

Little is known of John Standard's personal life, but he is credited with two inventions that people used daily: an improved refrigerator design (patent #455891) received on June 14, 1891, and an improved oil stove eight years later (patent #413689) on October 29, 1889.

The refrigerator. The refrigerator was already an existing invention, but Standard created a new configuration that improved their functioning and efficiency. His innovation also included an ice chamber for keeping foods cold.

The oil stove. Standard did not create the oil stove, but he made improvements to it: His patent included a design that saved space, allowing it to be used on trains to serve buffet style meals.

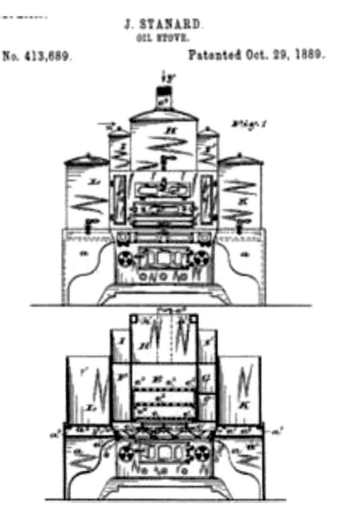

John Standard Oil Stove Patent (1889)

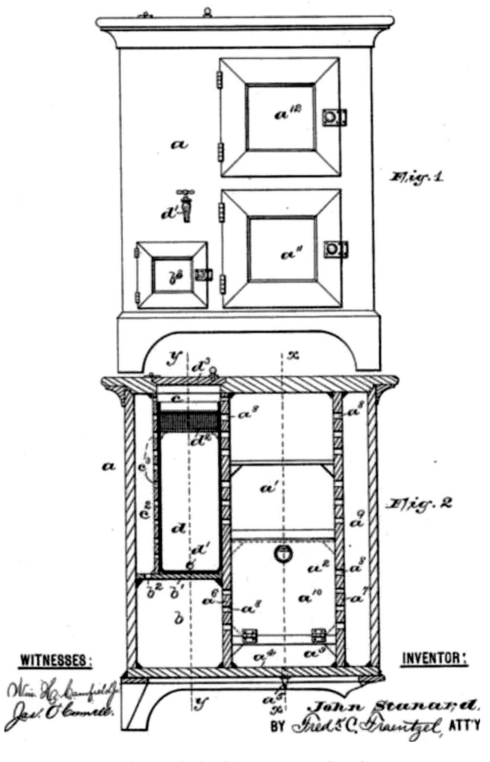

John Standard Refrigerator Patent (1891)

15. Madame CJ Walker (December 23, 1867 – May 25, 1919)

"I had to make my own living and my own opportunity. But I made it! Don't sit down and wait for the opportunities to come. Get up and make them." Madame CJ Walker

Sarah Breedlove McWilliams Walker (aka Madame Walker or Madame CJ Walker) was a pioneer for African American women's hair in the early 20th century.

Walker had an extremely difficult childhood. She was the youngest of six children, and the only one born free. The others were all enslaved, including her parents. Both her parents died when she was a young child: her mother died in 1872 from illness and her father remarried, but died a few years later.

At just seven years of age, Walker was an orphan.

She stayed with various relatives before moving in with an older sister and her husband. Unfortunately, she was abused by the husband, prompting her to run away. When she turned fourteen, she married Moses McWilliams.

Four years later, Walker became pregnant and had a daughter (Lelia). Tragedy would strike Walker again in 1887 when her husband Moses was reportedly killed by a white lynch mob.

After her husband's passing, Walker and her daughter moved to St. Louis, where they reunited with her brothers, who took them in. Her brothers were barbers and she worked as a laundrywoman.

Shortly after moving, Walker noticed her hair was starting to fall out. She had severe dandruff and other skin issues that affected her hair. This was common among African American women at the time, with many possible reasons why:

- Use of harsh products such as lye
- Poor diet
- Stress
- Illness
- Infrequent hair washing

Getting desperate, she tried many products that promised to save her hair, but nothing worked.

In 1904, Walker became a sales agent for Annie Minerva Turnbo Malone, another successful (and wealthy) African American entrepreneur.

Malone was born in Southern Illinois and was the daughter of slaves. After experimenting with various hair products, Malone created the Poro Company and the hit product "Wonderful Hair Grower." She eventually moved to St. Louis, where she met Walker.

The next year, Walker and her daughter moved to Denver, Colorado, and continued to sell products for Malone. Shortly after moving, she began to create her own hair care line as well. Walker eventually left the Poro Company and began to focus on building her own business.

In 1906, she married Charles Walker, a savvy businessman who helped her with advertising and promotion. (This is when she became known as Madame Walker and her daughter became A'Leila.) They began selling products door to door, and added a new aspect to Walker's business: teaching women of color how to take care of their hair. Later that year, the pair traveled the country, selling the products, while A'leila stayed home, handling the mail order operations.

In 1908, Walker and her husband moved to Pittsburgh, Pennsylvania and opened a beauty parlor and Leila College, which was a school to train their "hair culturists." The Denver office was closed shortly thereafter, and A'leila joined them in Pittsburgh, running the daily operations.

Walker continued to expand her business, moving her headquarters to Indianapolis, Indiana, then Harlem, New York in 1913.

Walker was very active in the African American community, contributing monies to the following institutions:

- Tuskegee Institute
- Bethel African American Methodist Episcopal Church
- Industrial Institute in Georgia
- Mary McLeod Bethune's Daytona Education and Industrial School for Negro Girls (which was later changed to Bethune-Cookman University)
- The Palmer Memorial Institute in North Carolina

In 1912, Walker attended the annual gathering of the National Negro Business League, telling the crowd:

"I am a woman who came from the cotton fields of the South. From there I was promoted to the washtub. From there, I was promoted to the cook kitchen. And from there, I promoted myself into the business of manufacturing hair goods and preparations. I have built my own factory on my own ground."

Did you know?

- Between 1911 and 1919, Walker employed several thousand women and trained 20,000 sales agents

- Her sales team sold products in the United States, Cuba, Jamaica, Haiti, Panama, and Costa Rica

- Walker raised funds to establish a branch of the YMCA in the Indianapolis black community

- Walker was believed to be the richest African American woman at the time of her death

- In 1993, Walker was inducted into the National Women's Hall of Fame in Seneca, New York

- The U.S. Postal Service issued a Madam Walker commemorative stamp in 1998

- The majority of people in leadership roles in her company were African American women

- Business tycoons John D. Rockefeller and Jay Gould were Walker's neighbors when she lived at the Vilia Lewaro in New York.

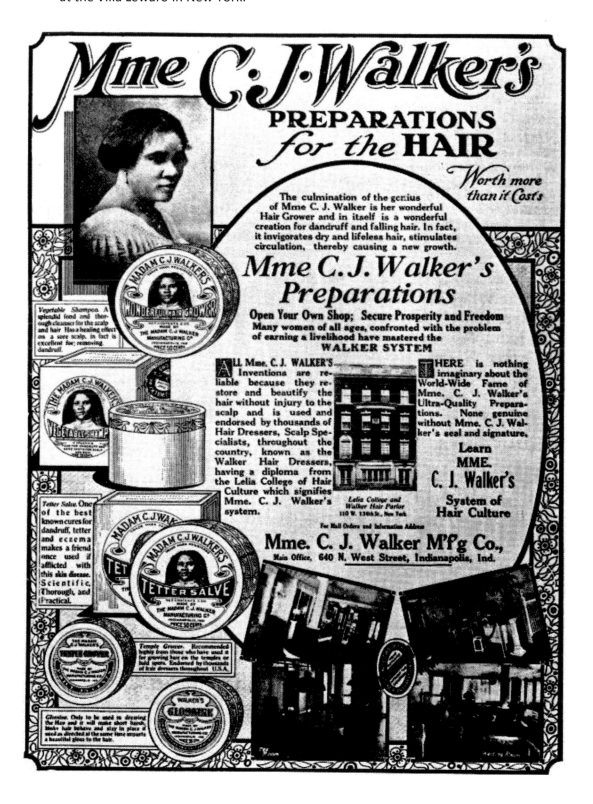

16. Granville T. Woods (April 23, 1856 – January 30, 1910)

"The Black Thomas Edison."

Granville T. Woods was born in Columbus, Ohio. He received formal schooling until age 10, when he had to drop out and work in a machine shop to help support his family.

Even though Woods had to quit school temporarily, he knew learning a skill was important. As a result, he made an effort to educate himself at every opportunity. The hard work paid off: Woods eventually became an engineer on the Danville and Southern Railroad in Missouri. He also became a fireman.

Even though this was quite an accomplishment, his desire to keep learning was still strong. In 1874, Woods moved to Springfield, Illinois, where he studied mechanical and electrical engineering in college. Once completed, he returned to Ohio, becoming an engineer with Dayton and Southwestern Railroad.

Not one to rest on his laurels, he knew there was more he could do. So, in 1880, he moved to Cincinnati, Ohio and created Woods Electric Company, as well as his mechanical engineering and inventor businesses.

Amazing Inventions

Woods really liked trains, and spent long hours looking for ways to improve them. Thanks to his ingenuity, the railroads became more efficient and safer. Even today, trains are still one of the best ways to transport goods and services across the country as well as around the world.

Woods has a long list of inventions, including the following:

The Telegraphony. On April 17, 1885, Woods patented the "telegraphony" (patent #315368), which was a combination of a telephone and telegraph. This device allowed a telegraph station to send voice and telegraph messages over a single wire. He later sold the rights for the device to American Bell Telephone Company.

Synchronous Multiplex Railway Telegraph. Patented by Woods on November 15, 1887, (patent #373383), this device allowed for communications between train stations and moving trains. This invention is not without controversy: Thomas Edison eventually filed a motion claiming ownership of this patent, saying he created a similar telegraph first. (Edison filed two motions, but both were denied.)

Other notable inventions by Woods include the following:

- **Steam Boiler Furnace** (Patent #299894) June 3, 1884
- **Overhead Conducting System for Electric Railway** (Patent #383844) May 29, 1888
- **Electric Railway System** (Patent #463020) November 10, 1891
- **Automatic Air Brake** (Patent #701981) June 10, 1902

Did you know?

- Granville Woods had over 60 patents

- Many of his products were sold to Westinghouse, General Electric, and American Engineering

Granville Electric Railway Conduit Patent (1893)

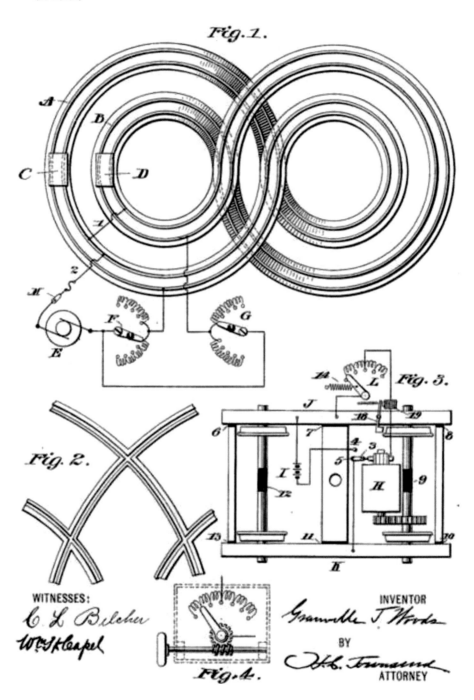

Granville T. Woods Amusement Apparatus Patent (1889)

Section II: The Politicians.

African Americans have been active in the United States' political system since the 1800's. By participating in the political process, citizens can let their voices be heard and make changes from the inside out, using the laws to their advantage.

Marching and peacefully protesting in the streets is a great way to bring awareness to various issues that are deemed important. However, that's just one piece of the puzzle. It's critical to have judges, congressmen, attorneys and other influential politicians in positions to *make* those changes.

1. Carol Mosely Braun (August 16, 1947 -)

"If we can rebuild Iraq, we can rebuild Illinois and Indiana. And if we can do Baghdad, we can do Baltimore.

"Magic lies in challenging what seems impossible." Carol Mosley Braun

Carol Mosely Braun goes down in history as the first female African American Senator, serving from 1993 to 1999.

Braun was born and raised in Chicago, Illinois, and attended Parker High School (now known as Paul Robeson). After a brief stint at the University of Illinois at Urbana- Champaign, she earned her Bachelor's Degree in political science at the University of Illinois Chicago campus in 1969. Braun furthered her education by earning a Juris Doctor (JD) degree (a professional degree in law) from the University of Chicago Law School in 1972.

After graduating, Braun worked as a prosecutor in the United States Attorney's office in Chicago from 1973 to 1977. Her specialties were civil law, appellate law, housing, health policy and environmental law.

In 1999, President Bill Clinton nominated Braun to be the United States Ambassador to New Zealand, and in 2004, she ran for President of the United States.

Did you know?

- Braun won the Attorney General's Special Achievement Award

- In 1993, Braun convinced the Senate Judiciary Committee to stop plans to renew a design patent for the United Daughters of Confederacy, because it contained the Confederate flag

- Braun is an honorary member of Delta Sigma Theta Sorority Incorporated

- Braun launched a line of organic food products (Ambassador Organics)

- Braun is the first woman to serve on the Senate Finance Committee

2. Thurgood Marshall (July 2, 1908 – January 24, 1993)

"I wish I could say that racism and prejudice were only distant memories. We must dissent from the indifference. We must dissent from the apathy. We must dissent from the fear, the hatred and the mistrust…. We must dissent because America can do better, because America has no choice but to do better." Thurgood Marshall

Thurgood Marshall is the first African American to serve on the on the United States Supreme Court as an Associate Justice (the highest court in the land).

The Supreme Court has jurisdiction over all state and federal court cases involving issues of federal law. It also has the final say when dealing with federal laws and the U.S. Constitution. All justices are nominated by the President of the United States and confirmed by the Senate. Once appointed to the Supreme Court, justices serve for life, unless they decide to resign, retire, or are removed via impeachment.

Prior to being appointed to the Supreme Court, Marshall was a powerful civil rights attorney, playing a crucial role in the advancement of rights for African Americans.

Marshall was born in Baltimore, Maryland. His great-grandfather was a slave, captured from the Democratic Republic of the Congo.

His father (William Marshall) was a railroad porter and his mother (Norma Marshall) was a school teacher. Both parents believed in the importance of education, and introduced him to the U.S. Constitution and the various laws of the country at an early age.

Marshall graduated with honors from Lincoln University with a Bachelors of Arts degree in Humanities, with a minor in American literature and philosophy. He went on to study law at Howard University, graduating first in his class in 1933. While in college, he took a stronger interest in discrimination against African Americans, and wondered how the law could be used to fight it.

After graduating law school, Marshall returned to Baltimore and started his own law firm. He eagerly joined the National Association for the Advancement of Colored People (NAACP) and represented the organization in many discrimination suit cases.

Before being appointed to the Supreme Court, Marshall was involved in many landmark cases that affected the rights of many African Americans:

- **Shelley v. Kraemer.** In 1945, the Shelley's, an African American family, purchased a home in St. Louis, Missouri. However, they did not realize there was a restrictive covenant placed on the house in 1911. The covenant declared *"people of the Negro or Mongolian Race"* were prohibited from occupying the property. Louis Kraemer, (who lived 10 blocks away), sued to prevent the Shelley's from moving in.

Marshall was the head of the NAACP Legal Defense and Educational Fund at the time, and argued the case in front of the Supreme Court. He won the suit in 1948 (along with African American attorney George L. Vaughn).

The Supreme Court cited the Fourteenth Amendment, which guarantees individual rights, and that equal protection of the law cannot be achieved with inequalities:

"The owners of the properties were willing sellers, and contracts of sale were accordingly consummated. It is clear that, but for the active intervention of the state courts, supported by the full panoply of state power, petitioners would have been free to occupy the properties in question without restraint."

- **Murray v. Pearson.** In 1934, Donald Gaines Murray, an African American college graduate, attempted to enroll in the University of Maryland Law School, but was rejected due to segregation. Marshall took the case and argued the rule was unlawful, violating the *"separate but equal"* ruling of Plessy v. Ferguson. The state did not did not provide a comparable curriculum at a state-run African American college, so Mr. Murray should be able to attend. The Maryland Court of Appeals ruled against the state of Maryland, giving Marshall the victory.

- **Brown v Board of Education.** In 1951, a class-action suit was filed by Oliver L. Brown against the Topeka, Kansas Board of Education. The suit challenged the notion of separate but equal, claiming the accommodations, services and treatment of African American students was inferior to their white counterparts.

  The case eventually made its way to the Supreme Court, where Justice Marshall led a suit, demanding an immediate reversal of its policy of racial discrimination. In 1954, the Supreme Court ruled in favor of Brown, stating *"separate educational facilities are inherently unequal."*

Did you know?

- Justice Marshall was a member of Alpha Phi Alpha Fraternity Incorporated

- Langston Hughes and Cab Calloway were Marshall's classmates at Lincoln University

- Justice Marshall won an astounding 29 of 32 cases he took before the Supreme Court

- A painting of Thurgood Marshall hangs in the White House

- In 1980, The University of Maryland School of Law named their new library the Thurgood Marshall Law Library

- The Baltimore-Washington Airport was renamed the Baltimore-Washington International Thurgood Marshall Airport on October 1, 2005, and was ranked the best airport of its size in the world by the Airports Council International in 2010

- The movie *Marshal,* highlighting the landmark Brown vs Board of Education case was released in October 2017

3. Barack H. Obama II (August 4, 1961 -)

"Change will not come if we wait for some other person or some other time. We are the ones we've been waiting for. We are the change that we seek."

"Our destiny is not written for us, but by us." Barack Obama

Barack Hussein Obama made history, becoming the first African American President of the United States. Obama served two terms as the 44th President, from 2009 to 2017.

Obama was born and raised in Honolulu, Hawaii, but spent four years in Indonesia as a young child.

After graduating from Columbia University with a BA in political science in 1983, Obama worked briefly as a financial researcher and writer at Business International Corporation.

In 1985, Obama became the director of the Developing Communities Project in Chicago. While there, he established a job training program, college prep tutoring program, and tenants' rights organization in the Altgeld Gardens housing project.

In 1988, Obama decided to continue his studies, enrolling in Harvard Law School. In the summers of 1989 and 1990, he worked as an associate at two Chicago Law firms: Sidney Austin and Hopkins & Sutter.

Obama graduated from Harvard in 1991 with a Juris Doctor (JD) degree magna cum laude, which means *"with great honor"*. He returned to Chicago and worked as Visiting Law and Government Fellow at the University Chicago Law School. The very next year, he began teaching constitutional law at the University of Chicago Law School.

Political Career

Obama's career as a politician began in 1996, when he was elected to the Illinois Senate. He was re-elected in 1998 and 2002. In 2002, when President Bush made a case for war in Iraq, Obama led an anti-Iraq war rally in Chicago.

In 2004, he was elected to the U.S. Senate and his popularity began to rise, especially after delivering a powerful speech at the Democratic National Convention, also in 2004. His speech received rave reviews, increasing the talk of him making a presidential run.

Obama was very active in the Senate, introducing or participating in many bills and amendments. One such amendment was the Defense Authorization Act of 2007, which added safeguards for personality-disorder military discharges. He also played a key role in an amendment to the State Children's Health Insurance Program, which provided one year of job protection for family members caring for soldiers with injuries caused by combat.

On February 10, 2007, Obama became a candidate for President of the United States. Selecting Joe Biden as his running mate, he defeated John McCain, claiming 365 electoral votes to McCain's 173. (He needed 270 votes to win). Obama also won 52.9% of the popular vote, making him the 44th President of the United States.

During his presidency, Obama enacted many laws and initiated various programs, including the following:

Stimulus package. On February 17, 2009, Obama signed the American Recovery and Investment Act. Valued at $787 billion, the package was designed to help the country recover from a major recession.

Auto Industry. Chrysler and General Motors were on the verge of bankruptcy, also in 2009. To avert this crisis, Obama renewed government loans for both automakers, allowing them to stay in business while reorganizing.

NASA. In 2010, the program shifted focus under Obama's leadership, with an increased emphasis on research and developing future manned missions to Mars.

Supreme Court. Obama appointed two women to the Supreme Court, including the first Hispanic Justice, Sonia Sotomayor on May 26, 2009. That increased the number of women on the court to 3, the first time ever on the Supreme Court.

LGBT rights. In 2013, Obama urged the Supreme Court to rule in favor of same-sex marriage. In 2015, the Supreme Court obliged, saying same-sex marriage was a fundamental right.

Affordable Care Act. Also known as Obama Care, the ACA was a major overhaul of the U.S. health care system. Signed into law on March 23, 2010, two key features of the plan included guaranteed health insurance to cover the uninsured and prohibiting the denial of coverage based on pre-existing conditions.

Osama Bin Laden. Osama Bin Laden was the mastermind behind the September 11, 2001 terrorist attacks in New York and Washington, D.C. A massive, world-wide manhunt to locate Bin Laden after the attacks was conducted, but was unsuccessful. In 2011, he was finally found, hiding in Abbottabad, Pakistan.

After deliberating with his top advisors, Obama ordered a surprise, pre-dawn raid on Bin Laden's compound. U.S. Navy Seals stormed the hideaway, catching him and his guards by surprise. After a short battle, Bin Laden was killed. The raid was deemed a success, prompting celebrations around the world.

Cuba. After several friendly meetings between the United States and Cuba, the two countries agreed to restore relations after nearly 60 years in 2013. Obama became the first sitting U.S. President to visit the country since 1928.

When Obama left office in January 2017, his approval rating was an impressive 60%.

Did you know?

- Obama's father earned a Master of Arts (M.A.) degree in economics from Harvard University, while his mother received a Ph.D. in anthropology

- Obama went to school in Indonesia from age's six to ten

- In 1989, Michelle Robinson declined several of Obama's requests to go out on a date before she finally accepted. They married in 1992 and have two daughters: Malia and Sasha

- High school classmates called Obama "Barry"

- Obama was elected the first black president of the Harvard Law Review

- In 1992, Obama led a voter registration campaign in Illinois, registering 150,000 unregistered African American voters

- Obama worked for Davis, Miner, Barnhill & Galland, a law firm specializing in civil rights from 1993 to 2004

- Obama won the Nobel Peace Prize in 2009

4. Hiram Revels (September 27, 1827 – January 16, 1901)

"I am true to my own race. I wish to see all done that can be done for their encouragement to assist them in acquiring property, in becoming intelligent, enlightened, useful, valuable citizens". Hiram Revels

During Reconstruction, Hiram Revels was sent by the Mississippi State Legislature to fill a vacancy in the U.S. Senate from 1870 to 1871. This made him the first-ever African American Senator in U.S. history.

Revels was born to free parents in Fayetteville, North Carolina. Even though it was illegal for black children to receive an education at the time in North Carolina, he went to a school taught by a woman of color who was also free. After a few years of schooling, Revels became a barber.

A few years later, he decided to continue his education, attending the Beech Grove Quaker Seminary in Liberty, Indiana. In 1857, he became a student at the Darke County Seminary for black students in Ohio.

In 1861, Revels' life took an unexpected turn: When the Civil War started, he helped organize two regiments of African American troops in Maryland. Two years later in 1863, he helped recruit African American soldiers in Missouri. These actions (combined with being an ordained minister) eventually led him to become a Union chaplain.

After the Civil war ended, Revels moved to Natchez, Mississippi. Once settled, he joined the African Methodist Episcopal Church, and was elected alderman in 1868. Becoming an alderman eventually led him to being elected as the first African American member of the U.S. Senate.

Southern Democrats resisted his acceptance into the Senate, but Revels' supporters (northern whites and African Americans) were able to help him keep his seat.

Did you know?

- Senator Revels was president of Alcorn College, the first land grant college for black students

- Senator Revels was married and had six daughters

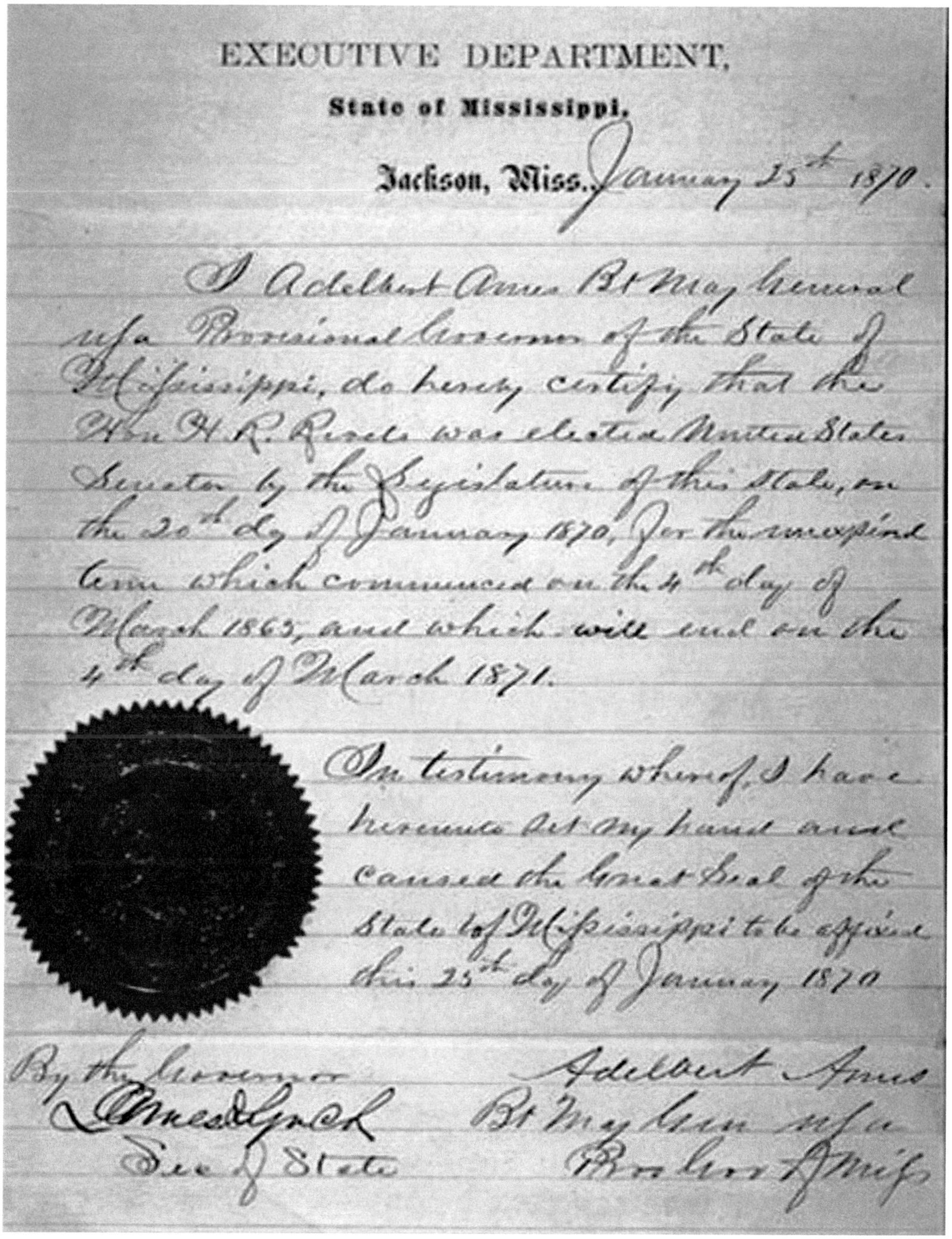

EXECUTIVE DEPARTMENT,
State of Mississippi.
Jackson, Miss. January 25th 1870.

I Adelbert Ames Bt Maj General USA Provisional Governor of the State of Mississippi, do hereby certify that the Hon H. R. Revels was elected United States Senator by the Legislature of this State, on the 20th day of January 1870, for the unexpired term which commenced on the 4th day of March 1865, and which will end on the 4th day of March 1871.

In testimony whereof, I have hereunto set my hand and caused the Great Seal of the State of Mississippi to be affixed this 25th day of January 1870

By the Governor
James D. Lynch
Sec of State

Adelbert Ames
Bt Maj Gen USA
Pro Gov of Miss

Revels Senate confirmation letter (1870)

5. Condoleezza Rice (November 14, 1954 -)

"Self-esteem comes from achievements. Not from lax standards and false praise."

"You never cede control of your own ability to be successful to something called racism." Condoleezza Rice

Condoleezza Rice was the 66th Secretary of State of the United States. She's also the first African American woman to serve in this important role. (The first African American was General Colin Powell, who served from 2001 to 2005.)

The Secretary of State is nominated by the President, and is responsible for foreign policy. Along with the Secretary of the Treasury, Secretary of Defense, and Attorney General, this high-ranking position is considered one of the four most important Cabinet positions in the United States government.

Rice was appointed by President George W. Bush, and advised him on issues related to U.S. foreign policy. Other duties she was responsible for included the following:

- Negotiate, interpret or terminate treaties relating to foreign affairs

- Supervised the enforcement of U.S. immigration policies abroad

- "Personally participates in or directs U.S. representatives to international conferences, organizations, and agencies"

Rice was born in Birmingham, Alabama when racial segregation was prevalent. Her name Condoleezza comes from the term *"con dolcezza,"* which means *"with sweetness"* in Italian.

Rice's parents were very keen on education. Her mother (Angelena Rice) was a high school science teacher, and her father (John Wesley Rice, Jr.) was a high school guidance counselor and Presbyterian minister.

When Rice was three years old, she was learning to speak French, and was introduced to music, figure skating and ballet. She graduated from high school at age 16, and attended the University of Denver, where she aspired to be a concert pianist. While in college, she abruptly changed her mind about becoming a pianist and decided to focus on political science. She went on to graduate from college at age 19 with a B.A. in political science.

Rice continued her studies, and at the age of 26, received her Ph.D. in political science from the Josef Korbel School of International Studies, at the University of Denver. (Ph.D. stands for Doctor of Philosophy, which is the highest degree in the liberal arts program.)

In 1981, Rice became an assistant professor of political science at Stanford University. In 1987, she was promoted to associate professor.

Rice's political career began after an arms control experts meeting at Stanford in 1985. Brent Scowcroft, President Gerald Ford's National Security Advisor at the time, was slated to join George Bush's cabinet once he took office. He asked Rice to become his Soviet Union "expert" on the United States Security Council once he assumed his new role.

Upon meeting Rice, newly elected President Bush was very impressed with her knowledge and expertise on Russian affairs. He began to seek her advice on how to deal with Russian leaders Mikhail Gorbachev and Boris Yeltsin, which she obliged.

Rice eventually returned to Stanford, and in 1993, she was appointed as Stanford's Provost (chief budget and academic officer) and full professor. Rice is the first female, first African American, and youngest provost in Stanford's history.

On December 17, 2000, Rice stepped down as provost when she was named National Security Advisor. This position made her the chief advisor to the U.S. government on matters of security. She was named Secretary of State in 2005.

Did you know?

- Rice studied Russian at Moscow State University

- A 15 year old Rice played Mozart with the Denver Symphony

- Rice has appeared on the Time 100: the magazine's list of the world's most influential people four times

- Rice grew up a democrat, but changed to republican in 1982 when she disagreed with Jimmy Carter's foreign policy

- Chevron named a 129,000 ton supertanker after Rice in 1993: the SS Condoleezza Rice

In Memoriam:

Dick Gregory (October 12, 1932 – August 19, 2017)

If you don't program your mind, it will be programmed for you."

"One of the things I keep learning is that the secret of being happy is doing things for other people."
Dick Gregory

Dick Gregory was a man who wore many hats. Over his illustrious life and career, he was a comedian, civil rights activist and entrepreneur.

Richard Claxton Gregory (aka Dick Gregory) was born into poverty in St. Louis, Missouri. He attended Sumner High School and was a member of the track team. Gregory ran well enough to earn a scholarship to Southern Illinois University in 1951. His college career was interrupted in 1954 when was drafted into the U.S. Army.

Gregory served for eighteen months and returned to SIU, but dropped out shortly thereafter in 1956. Later, Gregory would say they *"didn't want me to study, they wanted me to run."*

While in the Army, Gregory found his true calling: A commanding officer suggested he try comedy as he was great at telling jokes.

Gregory moved to Chicago in 1958. He worked for the United States Postal Service during the day and performed at local comedy clubs at night. While many African American comediennes stayed with safer material, Gregory pushed the envelope, finding humor in current events:

- *"I've been reading so much about cigarettes and cancer, I quit reading."*

- *"I sat in at a lunch counter for nine months. When they finally integrated, they didn't have what I wanted."*

- *"We tried to integrate a restaurant, and they said, "We don't serve colored folk here," and I said "Well I don't eat colored folk nowhere. Bring me some pork chops."*

In 1961, Gregory got his first big break: While working at the Roberts Bar in Chicago, he caught the attention of Hugh Hefner, who was in attendance. Hefner liked Gregory so much, he hired him on the spot to work at the Chicago Playboy Club.

As Gregory's popularity began to rise, so did the demand for him to make various guest appearances. Gregory was asked to perform on the hit television show *Tonight Starring Jack Paar.* Appearing on this show would give Gregory the exposure he desperately needed, but he declined the offer. Not, once but several times.

A confused Paar would eventually call Gregory, asking him why he kept refusing to come on the show. Gregory told them he would not appear because African American comics could *perform,* but they were never asked to sit on the couch and be *interviewed* afterwards.

Gregory declined to be on the show until he could sit and converse with Paar like other guests. The show's producers eventually agreed, allowing Gregory to stay after his performance and talk to Paar, live on air.

Gregory became the first African American to sit on the famous couch and be interviewed.

As America moved into the 1960's, Gregory began to combine comedy and social commentary with increasing frequency. He also voiced his opinion on several major issues:

- He publicly opposed the Vietnam War

- He believed the Census Bureau purposely undercounted minorities

- He led fund raisers to feed hungry people in Marks, Mississippi

- He traveled overseas to support various causes:

    - **France.** Protested the French involvement in Indo-China
    - **Northern Ireland.** Advised Irish Republican Army political protestors
    - **Ethiopia.** Fought against world hunger
    - **Tehran.** Went on hunger strike in an attempt to negotiate the American hostage's release

As the years went by, Gregory became even more outspoken on political matters:

On Women's Equality Day (August 26, 1978), Gregory spoke out in support of feminists, joining Gloria Steinem and others on the National ERA March for Ratification and Extension. The group of over 100,000 marched to the U.S. Capitol, demanding a deadline extension for the proposed Equal Rights Amendment. The march was a success, with the deadline being extended to June 30, 1982.

In addition to his political activism, Gregory became health conscious as well, changing his diet and striving to improve the overall health and life-expectancy of African Americans.

In 1981, Gregory embarked on what he called *"the longest medically supervised scientific fast in the history of the planet."* Under the supervision of doctors at Dillard University's Flint- Goodridge Hospital, Gregory consumed only a gallon of water daily for seventy consecutive days.

The experiment was called the "Dick Gregory's Zero Nutrition Fasting Experiment". He ate no food and focused on drinking water and praying. At the end of the experiment, a healthy and exuberant Gregory traveled by foot from New Orleans to Baton Rouge, Louisiana, a distance of approximately 100 miles.

In 1984, Gregory founded Health Enterprises, Inc. One of his featured products was the powdered drink mix "Slim-Safe Bahamian Diet". In 1985, the Ethiopian government endorsed the product, claiming it was a success. In 2014, Gregory created the "Caribbean Diet for Optimal Health".

Dick Gregory died in Washington D.C. on August 29, 2017, at the age of 84. He was survived by his wife Lilian Smith and their ten children.

Upon hearing of his death, friends, fans and celebrities around the world paid their respects via social media:

"Humanity has lost a Giant. RIP my dear friend." Cicely Tyson

"I've known Dick Gregory since I was 16 years old. A true, committed, and consistent freedom fighter. May he Rest in Peace." Al Sharpton

"Dick Gregory lived an amazing, revolutionary life. A groundbreaker in comedy and a voice for justice. RIP." John Legend

Did you know?

- Gregory was a member of Alpha Phi Alpha Fraternity Incorporated

- Gregory received the Outstanding Athlete Award at Southern Illinois University in 1953

- Gregory was ranked number 82 on Comedy Central's list of the 100 Greatest Stand-ups of all time

- Gregory has a star on the St. Louis Walk of Fame

- Gregory ran for mayor of Chicago in 1967 and President of the United States in 1968 as a write-in candidate of the Freedom and Peace Party

- Gregory appeared in over a dozen films and television shows, wrote over a dozen books and has over a dozen comedy albums

Puzzles and Word Games

Puzzles and word games are very entertaining for both adults and children of all ages. Adults like them for the mental stimulation, while they are an excellent way for children to learn and retain information. Parents can also use puzzles as a fun way to educate their children.

On the next few pages are challenging word puzzles and questions about the amazing African Americans discussed in this book. Give them a try!

1. **Test Your Memory**

1. Which inventor was made an honorary member of the International Association of Firefighters?

   _____

2. Who worked for NACA and what does it stand for?

   _____

3. How long did Benjamin Banneker's clock function without breaking down?

   _____

4. Where did Barack Obama teach constitutional law?

   _____

5. What are the 8 Cardinal Virtues created by George Washington Carver?

   1. _____

   2. _____

   3. _____

   4. _____

   5. _____

   6. _____

   7. _____

   8. _____

6. Who received the first U.S. patent as an African American? What was it for? What was the date?

_____

7. Who received their Ph.D. from the University of Denver at the age of 26?

_____

8. Who is the first African American woman to serve on the Senate Finance Committee?

_____

9. Who created the Laserphaco Probe? What does it do?

_____

_____

10. Who was inducted into the National Inventors Hall of Fame in 2003?

_____

11. How long was Dick Gregory's medically supervised fast in 1981?

_____

12. Why was the American Recovery and Investment Act signed by President Obama in 2009?

_____

13. Who started high school at age 10 and graduated at age 14?

_____

14. Who created the fountain pen? What was their reason for creating it?

_____

15. What is the "Love sharpener?" When was it invented?

_____

16. Who was thought to be the *"wealthiest colored man in the Northwest?"* What did he invent?

   _____

17. What entrepreneur sold products across the United States and in Cuba, Jamaica, Haiti, Panama, and Costa Rica?

   _____

18. How many cases did Thurgood Marshall take before the U.S. Supreme Court? How many did he win?

   _____

19. What honor did Chevron bestow upon Condoleezza Rice?

   _____

20. How many patents does Granville Woods own? Who did he sell many of his inventions to?

   _____

21. What happened at Moon's Lake House?

   _____

22. Why did Dick Gregory refuse to appear on the Tonight Show with Jack Paar?

   _____

23. What year(s) was the first African American elected to the United States Senate?

   _____

24. Why did Tomas Elkins invent the ironing table?

_____

25. Which branch of the U.S. military named a cargo ship after Charles Drew? What was the date?

_____

26. Who is Elizabeth Jennings? What happened to her, and who defended her in court?

_____

#2.

Find the Inventor and Inventions

```
R D O O H E K O M S D S U M S
O F I W G P S R C C N R C M P
T O A Z Z E E L O D N O C Q E
A U R A U P L J J T C I R R C
V N R E F R I G E R A T O R T
E T U A Z U M R G T Q A A E R
L A A M C M R O E N U S B Q O
E I L A D V E K C K A N K H G
M N M B R M D X N N E O A J R
X P A O P B N R W G Q N N E A
R E N E P R A H S L I C N E P
S N A T F U X R E V R A C A H
D I C K G R E G O R Y D C Q B
O G B K T K L S A R A T O G A
L T G M V Y A W E R B P G Z K
```

ALEXANDERMILES – ALMANAC – BANNEKER - CARVER

CONDOLEEZZA – DICKGREGORY – ELEVATOR - FOUNTAINPEN

NASA – OBAMA – PEANUT - PENCILSHARPENER

REFRIGERATOR – SARATOGA – SMOKEHOOD - SPECTROGRAPH

Hint: Words can be left, right, up, down, diagonal or backwards

3. African American Crossword Puzzle

Across	Down
4. Movie made about her life	1. Supreme Court Justice
9. Inducted into National Women's Hall of Fame	2. Secretary of State
10. Nickname for pencil sharpener	3. Created the fountain pen
11. Created the bloodmobile	5. Invented the image converter
	6. Created by Garrett A Morgan
	7. 44th President
	8. Stand-up comic

4. African American Double Puzzle

Unscramble each of the book-inspired clue words.
Copy the letters in the numbered cells to other cells with the same number.

TNPATE

TAHM

CEICSNE
6

RAMCAE

PENATU

NETREPRENRUE

NAOSERT

VEOTRALE

DOMCOME
5 4

NIICEMED
7   2

CAASTCTRA
3

CAPSE TLHEUST

NOAMOYRST
1

				W				
1	2	3	4	5	6	7		

5. Unscramble the Tiles to Reveal an Inspirational Message

#1:

W E R	K N O	D G E	P O	W L E	I S

#2:

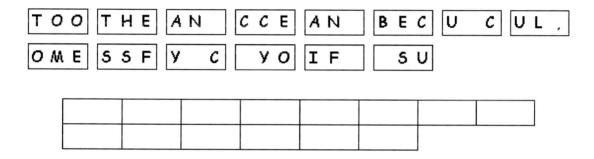

T O O	T H E	A N	C C E	A N	B E C	U C	U L ,
O M E	S S F	Y C	Y O	I F	S U		

#3:

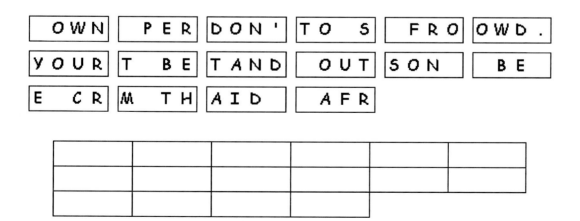

O W N	P E R	D O N '	T O S	F R O	O W D .
Y O U R	T B E	T A N D	O U T	S O N	B E
E C R	M T H	A I D	A F R		

6. Fallen Phrases

Unscramble the tiles to reveal a powerful, motivational message.

#1:

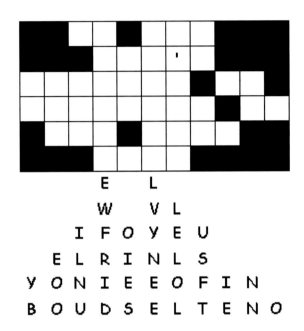

```
            E   L
        W       V   L
      I   F   O   Y   E   U
    E   L   R   I   N   L   S
  Y   O   N   I   E   E   O   F   I   N
  B   O   U   D   S   E   L   T   E   N   O
```

#2:

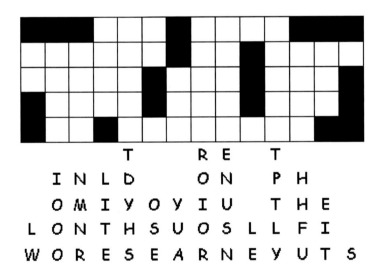

```
            T           R   E       T
    I   N   L   D           O   N       P   H
    O   M   I   Y   O   Y   I   U       T   H   E
  L   O   N   T   H   S   U   O   S   L   L   F   I
  W   O   R   E   S   E   A   R   N   E   Y   U   T   S
```

7. Word Search #2
Find the Inventor and Inventions

```
S  A  S  K  V  W  E  O  H  L  F  S  T  I  E
M  R  E  M  O  N  O  R  T  S  A  V  M  T  P
O  M  N  K  H  F  A  E  Z  D  M  A  N  R  O
K  F  A  T  F  T  L  I  H  V  G  E  O  M  C
E  O  T  V  C  E  A  U  C  E  D  T  O  A  S
H  E  O  C  S  E  B  C  I  N  B  O  N  O
O  P  R  C  L  B  Y  O  S  E  T  P  Q  P  R
O  L  O  K  B  P  N  E  V  I  C  I  U  L  C
D  P  I  L  C  V  R  N  O  L  F  N  L  R  I
E  N  L  J  E  P  I  L  O  R  A  C  Q  O  M
S  L  V  R  B  L  O  O  D  B  A  N  K  H  P
N  E  T  C  A  R  A  T  A  C  L  K  O  R  B
Y  E  H  A  I  R  C  A  R  E  K  E  L  A  R
R  L  K  H  U  R  B  M  E  A  Q  R  Y  Z  I
```

ASTRONOMER – BATH - BLOODBANK - CAROL –

CATARACT – ELKINS - HAIRCARE - IMAGECONVERTER –

INVENTOR – MICROSCOPE – POLITICIAN – PRESIDENT –

SENATOR – SMOKEHOOD – TELESCOPE

Hint: Words can be left, right, up, down, diagonal or backwards

8. Guess What? (Cryptogram)

#1

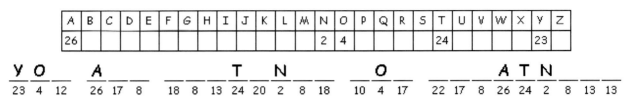

#2

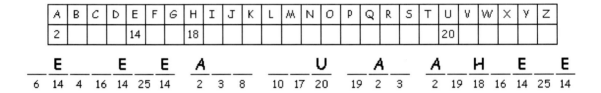

#3:

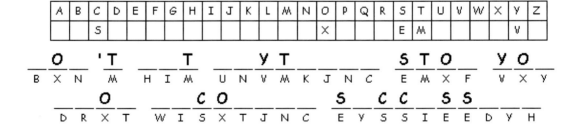

Answers

1. Test Your Memory

1. Garrett A Morgan (p.35)

2. Katherine Johnson: National Advisory Committee for Aeronautics (p. 30)

3. 40 years (p. 10)

4. The University of Chicago Law School (p. 53)

5. The 8 Cardinal Virtues (p. 20)
   - Always be considerate of women, children, and older people.
   - Be too brave to lie.
   - Be too generous to cheat.
   - Take your share of the world and let others take theirs.
   - Be clean both inside and out.
   - Neither look up to the rich nor down on the poor.
   - Lose, if need be, without squealing.
   - Win without bragging.

6. Thomas Jennings - March 3rd, 1821 – Dry scouring process (p. 29)

7. Condoleezza Rice (p. 58)

8. Carol Mosely Braun (p. 50)

9. Dr. Patricia Bath - dissolves cataracts with a laser quickly and with little pain. It also cleans the eye and allows a new lens to be easily inserted into the eye. (p. 13)

10. George Carruthers (p. 17)

11. 70 days (p. 61)

12. The package, valued at $787 billion, was designed to help the country recover from a major recession. (p. 54)

13. Katherine Johnson (p. 30)

14. William Purvis - *"the object of my invention is to provide a simple, durable, and inexpensive construction of a fountain pen adapted to general use and which may be carried in the pocket."* *(p. 39)*

15. Pencil sharpener - 11/23/1897 (p. 32)

16. Alexander Miles – the elevator (p. 33)

17. Madame CJ Walker (p. 44)

18. Marshall won an astounding 29 of 32 cases he took before the Supreme Court (p. 52)

19. Chevron named a 129,000 ton supertanker after her: the SS Condoleezza Rice (p. 59)

20. Granville Woods had over 60 sold to Westinghouse, General Electric, and American Engineering. (p. 47)

21. The potato chip was revolutionized, by either George Crum or his sister, Katie (p. 24)

22. Because African American comics could perform, but they were *never* asked to sit on the couch and be interviewed afterwards. (p. 61)

23. Hiram Revels was elected the first African American senator in the United States in 1870 and 1871. (p. 56)

24. This invention was ideal for those in cramped living spaces. (p. 27)

25. The U.S. Navy named a cargo ship the USNS Charles Drew, was christened and launched on February 27, 2010. (p. 25)

26. 1854, Elizabeth was forcibly removed from a streetcar and arrested. The case was represented in court by attorney Chester Arthur, who eventually became the 21st President of the United States. (p. 29)

2. Find the Inventor and Inventions (Answers)

Word Search #1 Solution

```
R D O O H E K O M S + + + + S
O F + + + + S + + + + + + + P
T O A Z Z E E L O D N O C + E
A U + + + + L + + + + + + + C
V N R E F R I G E R A T O R T
E T + A + + M R + T + + A + R
L A A M + + R + E + U S + + O
E I L A + + E + + K A N + + G
+ N M B + + D + + N E + A + R
+ P A O + + N + + + + N + E A
R E N E P R A H S L I C N E P
+ N A + + + X R E V R A C A H
D I C K G R E G O R Y + + + B
+ + + + + + L S A R A T O G A
+ + + + + + A + + + + + + + +
```

(Over, Down, Direction)

ALEXANDERMILES **(7, 15, N)**
ALMANAC **(3, 7, S)**
BANNEKER **(15, 13, NW)**
CARVER **(13, 12, W)**
CONDOLEEZZA **(13, 3, W)**
DICKGREGORY **(1, 13, E)**
ELEVATOR **(1, 8, N)**
FOUNTAINPEN **(2, 2, S)**
NASA **(10, 9, NE)**
OBAMA **(4, 10, N)**
PEANUT **(15, 11, NW)**
PENCILSHARPENER **(15, 11, W)**
REFRIGERATOR **(3, 5, E)**
SARATOGA **(8, 14, E)**
SMOKEHOOD **10, 1, W)**
SPECTROGRAPH **(15, 1, S)**

3. Crossword Puzzle Answers:

Across		Down	
4. HIDDEN FIGURES		1. THURGOODMARSHALL	
9. CJWALKER		2. CONDOLEEZZARICE	
10. LOVESHARPENER		3. WILLIAMPURVIS	
11. CHARLESDREW		5. GEORGECARRUTHERS	
		6. TRAFFICSIGNAL	
		7. BARACKOBAMA	
		8. DICKGREGORY	

4. African American Double Puzzle Answers:

Patent

TNPATE

Math

TAHM

Science

CEICSNE
6

Camera

RAMCAE

Peanut

PENATU

Entrepreneur

NETREPRENRUE

Senator

NAOSERT

Elevator

VEOTRALE

Commode

DOMCOME
5 4

Medicine

NIICEMED
7   2

Cataracts

CAASTCTRA
3

Space shuttle

CAPSE TLHEUST

Astronomy

NOAMOYRST
1

1	2	3		W		5	6	7
				4				

2nd puzzle answer: *"YES WE DID"*

5. Unscramble the Tiles to Reveal a Message (Answers)

#1.

W E R	K N O	D G E		P O	W L E		I S

"KNOWLEDGE IS POWER"

#2.

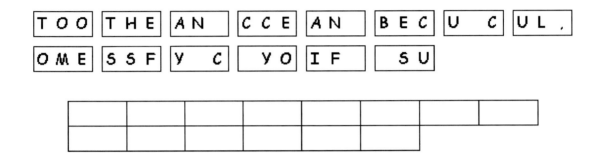

"IF THEY CAN BECOME SUCCESSFUL YOU CAN TOO"

#3.

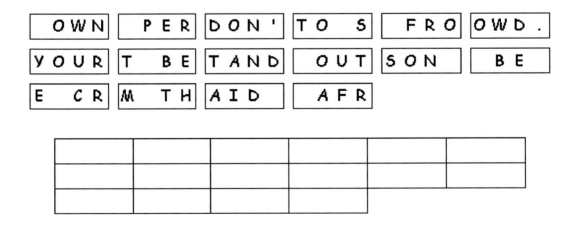

"DON'T BE AFRAID TO STAND OUT FROM THE CROWD. BE YOUR OWN PERSON."

6. Fallen Phrases (Answers)

#1.

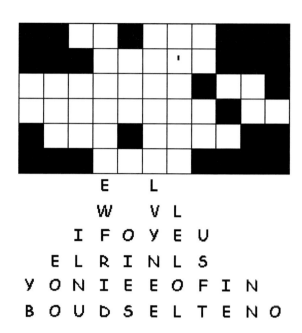

```
        E     L
      W    V  L
    I  F  O  Y  E  U
  E  L  R  I  N  L  S
Y  O  N  I  E  E  O  F  I  N
B  O  U  D  S  E  L  T  E  N  O
```

"IF YOU DON'T BELIEVE IN YORSELF, NO ONE ELSE WILL."

#2.

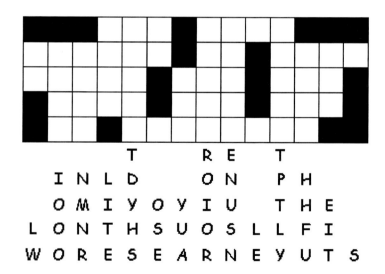

```
        T        R  E     T
    I  N  L  D        O  N     P  H
    O  M  I  Y  O  Y  I  U     T  H  E
  L  O  N  T  H  S  U  O  S  L  L  F  I
W  O  R  E  S  E  A  R  N  E  Y  U  T  S
```

"THE ONLY LIMITS IN THIS WORLD ARE THE ONES YOU PUT ON YOURSELF"

7. **Word Search #2 (Solution)**

```
S  +  S  +  +  +  +  +  +  +  +  +  +  I  E
M  R  E  M  O  N  O  R  T  S  A  +  M  T  P
O  +  N  +  H  +  A  E  +  +  +  A  N  R  O
K  +  A  +  +  T  L  I  +  +  G  E  O  +  C
E  +  T  +  +  E  A  +  C  E  D  T  +  +  S
H  +  O  +  S  E  +  B  C  I  N  +  +  +  O
O  +  R  C  L  +  +  O  S  E  T  +  +  +  R
O  +  O  K  +  +  N  E  V  +  +  I  +  +  C
D  P  I  +  +  V  R  N  +  +  +  +  L  +  I
E  N  +  +  E  P  I  L  O  R  A  C  +  O  M
S  +  +  R  B  L  O  O  D  B  A  N  K  +  P
+  +  T  C  A  R  A  T  A  C  +  +  +  +  +
+  E  H  A  I  R  C  A  R  E  +  +  +  +  +
R  +  +  +  +  +  +  +  +  +  +  +  +  +  +
+  +  +  +  +  +  +  +  +  +  +  +  +  +  +
```

(Over, Down, Direction)

ASTRONOMER (11,2,W)	**BATH** (8,6,NW)
BLOODBANK (5,11,E)	CAROL(12,10,W)
CATARACT (10,12,W)	ELKINS (6,6,SW)
HAIRCARE (3,13,E)	IMAGECONVERTER (14,1,SW)
INVENTOR (7,10,NE)	**MICROSCOPE** (15,10,N)
POLITICIAN (15,11,NW)	PRESIDENT (6,10,NE)
SENATOR (3,1,S)	SMOKEHOOD(1,1,S)
TELESCOPE 9,2,SW)	

8. Guess What? Cryptogram (Answers)

A	B	C	D	E	F	G	H	I	J	K	L	M	N	O	P	Q	R	S	T	U	V	W	X	Y	Z
17													2						7					22	

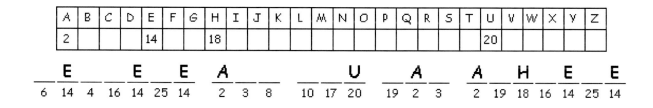

Y	_	_	A	_	_	_	_	T	_	N	_	_	_	_	_	_	A	T	N	_	_	_
22	3	1	17	26	19	14	19	25	7	21	2	19	14	13	3	26	15	26	19	17	7	2	19	25	25

"YOU ARE DESTINED FOR GREATNESS"

A	B	C	D	E	F	G	H	I	J	K	L	M	N	O	P	Q	R	S	T	U	V	W	X	Y	Z
2				14			18													20					

_	E	_	E	_	E	A	_	_	_	U	_	A	_	A	_	H	_	E	_	E
6	14	4	16	14	25	14	2	3	8	10	17	20	19	2	3	2	19	18	16	14	25	14

"BELIEVE AND YOU CAN ACHIEVE"

A	B	C	D	E	F	G	H	I	J	K	L	M	N	O	P	Q	R	S	T	U	V	W	X	Y	Z
		S												X			E	M						V	

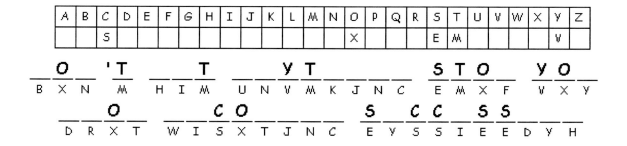

O	_	'T	_	T	_	_	Y	T	_	_	_	_	S	T	O	_	Y	O
B	X	N	M	H	I	M	U	N	V	M	K	J	N	C	E	M	X	F	V	X	Y

_	O	_	_	C	O	_	S	_	C	C	_	S	S	_	_
D	R	X	T	W	I	S	X	T	J	N	C	E	Y	S	S	I	E	E	D	Y	H

"DON'T LET ANYTHING STOP YOU FROM BECOMING SUCCESSFUL"

Closing Remarks

When I was eight years old, my mother made me do schoolwork every summer. While my friends were outside having the most fun in the history of mankind, I was stuck in the house, reading the Encyclopedia Britannica, writing book reports, and practicing my typing skills on the old typewriter.

I was also reading about African Americans and their great accomplishments throughout history.

To say I hated it would be an understatement. How could my mother be so mean? Why was she depriving me of all the fun I was supposed to be having with my friends? Did I do something wrong? Why was I being punished? Who cares about all these "old people?" I don't!

Fast forward forty years. As I reflect, I am ETERNALLY grateful that my mother (who was also a school teacher) made me read and write. She introduced me to people and events that weren't talked about in school. Thanks to her, I grew up knowing a lot more about things they didn't talk about in the classroom, especially topics dealing with African American history. I knew we were much more than Martin Luther King Jr. and Rosa Parks. Great as they are, I knew that was just the tip of the iceberg.

It was her insistence that I write book reports that gave me the idea to include interactive activities in the back of this book. They are a great way to retain what you've read.

Knowing these (and many other inventions) are made by African Americans can accomplish several things:

1. It can instill a sense of pride and self-worth in African Americans of all ages, especially young people;

2. It can inspire people to achieve the impossible;

3. It can help bring widespread awareness to the amazing contributions by African Americans.

There are many historical facts and contributions made by people of **all** races, creeds and colors that are not mentioned in traditional history books. In other words, there's a tremendous amount of knowledge and achievement that is not being passed down to the next generation. That's a disservice to us all.

As a society, it's we MUST recognize contributions of *everyone* who made this country great, not just a select few. Anything less is unacceptable.

I hope this book serves as an inspiration to whoever reads it. Let this book motivate you to accomplish things that no one thinks you can. Many of the heroes in this book succeeded against tremendous odds. Why can't you do the same? If they can, you can too. All you have to do is believe.

The title of this book is *"YES WE DID!"* But as you look in the mirror, say *"YES I CAN!"* Say it like you mean it!

We ALL have a talent. We ALL are capable of greatness. All you have to do is believe. I believe in you, and look forward to writing about *YOUR* accomplishments one day.

Thanks for reading! God Bless. Jeff White.

Coming Soon:

YES WE DID! The Art Edition by David Sanders

Thomas Elkins

Coming Soon:

YES WE DID! The Art Edition by David Sanders

Katherine Johnson

About the Artist

David Sanders is owner of Cross2infinity art studios. He was born in 1970 in Winona, Mississippi. His family moved to Chicago while he was still an infant. He developed a love for art and comics at the age of seven and has pursued it ever since. Honing his craft under the tutelage of Mr. Sherman Beck at Dunbar high school, David won awards for logo design and is still creating great art and comics today. His specialty is portraits, graphic design, and digital and wet mediums.

About the Author

Jeffrey White is a former financial advisor turned best-selling author, freelance writer, wellness coach, triathlete and personal trainer. He lives in Florida with his wife Monica and son Little Jeffrey. He is from Chicago, Illinois and graduated from Illinois State University with a degree in Business Administration. www.JeffWhiteFitnessSolutions.com

https://www.youtube.com/user/JWFitness1

Jeffrey has written several self-help and inspirational books, designed to help a person become the best they can be in several key aspects of their lives:

<u>The 3 Pillars of Strength: Increasing Your Physical, Mental and Spiritual Fitness.</u>

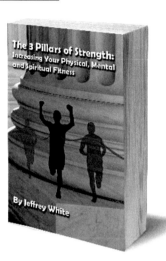

In order to become the best you can be, it's important to work on all aspects of your life, together. It's time for YOU to reach your FULL potential.

It's time to tap into ALL your unique traits and talents that can propel you to greatness.

It's time to face all the challenges and obstacles this world will throw at you with the quiet confidence that you CAN and WILL overcome.

It's time to understand that, at your disposal, you have the tools needed to succeed! Available in paperback, Audible and Kindle formats on Amazon.

<u>Readi - Set Go! A Simple Guide to Establishing a Successful Small Business.</u>

Co-written with Stephanie A. Wynn

Do you dream of owning your own business but don't know where to begin? Does the thought of being self-employed excite you, but scare you at the same time? Do you have an intense desire to run your own successful business? Are you tired of waiting on someone to give you a job and want to create one instead?

Starting a business is difficult, but it's not impossible. Gain valuable insight on the start-up process and running a successful business with this step by step guide. Learn about the critical first steps that many overlook when starting a business.

Are you READI to create a solid, reputable company that no one can take from you?

<u>**Success Principles 101: A Step By Step Guide on Setting and Achieving Goals.**</u>

The first book in the "Success" series: Are you ready for success? Setting goals is simple, accomplishing them is not. In this easy to read guide, we identify the pitfalls that many encounter while attempting to achieve their goals and how to overcome them.

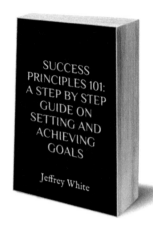

<u>**The Diet of Success: Healthy Eating Tips for Hard Working Professionals.**</u>

While many people think money is the key to happiness and prosperity, it's all irrelevant without good health. When it comes to success, many of us are willing to do anything to get it. Unfortunately, that often includes sacrificing our health and overall well-being.

The first line of defense against illness is not medicine from the doctor but the foods we eat. The effort it takes to be successful can take a tremendous toll on the body. By knowing which foods to eat (and avoid), a person can focus all their energies on setting and achieving goals instead of which medicines they need to take to make it through the day.

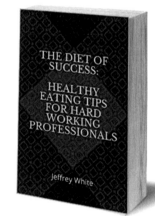

Cancer, diabetes, obesity, high blood pressure, and other ailments are near epidemic levels in today's society. Are pesticides, GMO's, artificial food colorings and other things added to our foods the culprit? Discover how many of the foods we eat today may be the reason behind so many of our health issues. Understand how a slight change in diet can not only keep us healthy, but provide the energy we need to achieve all our goals.

The foods we eat can either help us or hurt us. If you're working long hours and trying to make a better life for yourself, eating the proper foods can give you the energy not to make your dreams come true, but to let you enjoy the fruits of your labor for years to come.

Made in the USA
San Bernardino, CA
17 November 2017